Praise for *The Aesthetics of* Atheism

"*The Aesthetics of Atheism* demonstrates how our contemporary cultural imagination can become a source for significant theological and biblical inquiry. Readers will first be surprised and then convinced that TV horror stories like *Stranger Things*, the music of David Bowie and Leonard Cohen, and the art of Damien Hirst might actually open up the text of the Gospel of Mark in significant ways. Here is reflection on theology and contemporary culture at its finest. A provocative and groundbreaking book, *The Aesthetics of Atheism* will help readers explore the theological depths of the Gospel of Mark's depiction of the empty tomb, Jesus's cry on the cross, and the transfiguration by grounding their narratives in the cultural imagination. Callaway and Taylor want their readers to not only look at cultural images but to look through them."

—**Robert K. Johnston, Fuller Theological Seminary**

"Through Callaway and Taylor's analysis of popular cultural media, they present contemporary landmarks of a 'poetic of the numinous' that encompass the vast landscape of belief, unbelief, and everything in between. For this reason, *The*

Aesthetics of Atheism models a way to address existential realities with those more apt to find God on Netflix, at a concert, or in a gallery."

—Maria Fee, Fuller Theological Seminary

"In this courageous and creative work, Callaway and Taylor lead us beyond the tired binaries of modernity into honest engagement with our paradoxical existence and experience of God. In doing so, they've given us not only a fresh and challenging reading of the Gospel of Mark but have also provided a pathway toward receiving a/theistic popular culture as an aesthetic gift for revitalizing traditional construals of God's transcendence and immanence."

—Wesley Vander Lugt, lead pastor at Warehouse 242

"So often Christians desire to learn about a/theists as a means of converting them. There isn't anything inherently wrong with the motivations of that approach, but Callaway and Taylor propose another. Through the examination of the creative production of contemporary a/theism, this book is focused on walking along side a/theists and learning from them. It's not only a more respectful tone, it is more representational of what is really going on in our society—mutual growth. We are all on a journey. Let's understand one another and journey together. Callaway and Taylor touch on an important truth and do so in a beautiful and thoughtful way. By refusing to approach a/theism in a traditional (simplistic) way, they offer space to really consider it—and consider the camaraderie we all have in our response to our shared world. Creating this space is our best way forward in the post-Christian, post-truth world. Adopting Callaway and Taylor's posture will make it a world of possibilities."

—**Mike Davis, director of Leader Training and Resources, North Point Ministries**

"This is such an important work. Kutter Callaway and Barry Taylor are two of our most reliable cultural observers with sharp theological lenses. *The Aesthetics of Atheism* is the most important and powerful cultural analysis that I've come across in a long time. From *Stranger Things* to Damien Hirst, this book is brimming with astute observations and honest critiques of both theism and atheism."

—**Mako Fujimura, artist, director of Fuller Seminary's Brehm Center**

"'Absence makes the heart grow fonder,' or so they say. Maybe that's most true about God. For even the sincerest theists have sometimes encountered only darkness when they sought God; even Jesus felt forsaken in his cry of dereliction. When God hides, we tend to seek all the more. So then, what use is the paradox of derelict faith in a secular age? Kutter Callaway and Barry Taylor have weaved in this text a theological tapestry of resources for pinning oneself to that moment on the cross wherein, as they say, following G. K. Chesterton, 'God apostatizes against God's very self.' In our modern secular age, faith may continue to take on the shape of dereliction and we may need to squint our eyes in order to see the beauty of the Divine. And for those of us committed to the way of Jesus, you'll find Callaway and Taylor's evocative and critical theological commentary to be a lens that makes the squinting more bearable. We need books like this for times like this."

—**Evan Rosa, director of the Biola University Center for Christian Thought**

"Truth in advertising: I'm a fan of Kutter Callaway and Barry Taylor because they always ask provocative questions that make me think more deeply about my faith and how I live it. Bravo! This book would be a refreshing (perhaps 'sublime,' as they discuss the word) addition to any typical evangelism course in Christian colleges across the country."

—**Catherine Barsotti, Fuller Theological Seminary**

"Though it frustrates both my Christian and atheist friends, I find the forced dichotomy between atheist and theist to be simplistic. I'm thankful for folks like Kutter Callaway and Barry Taylor for imaging a world with more than two colors in our palate to create a shared reality."

—**Mike McHargue, cofounder** of *The Liturgists*, **host** of *Ask Science Mike*

The Aesthetics of Atheism

The Aesthetics of Atheism

Theology and Imagination in
Contemporary Culture

Kutter Callaway and Barry Taylor

Fortress Press
Minneapolis

THE AESTHETICS OF ATHEISM

Theology and Imagination in Contemporary Culture

Cover image: Abstract background/natrot/iStock.com

Cover design: Laurie Ingram

Print ISBN: 978-1-5064-3988-4

eBook ISBN: 978-1-5064-3989-1

The paper used in this publication meets the minimum requirements of American National Standard for Information Sciences — Permanence of Paper for Printed Library Materials, ANSI Z329.48-1984.

Manufactured in the U.S.A.

*to the women in our lives who sustain
our (lack of) faith*

Contents

Acknowledgments

Coauthored projects are, by definition, collaborative efforts, and this one is no exception. But a network of colleagues, students, and friends shaped our work in ways that made it something so much more than it would have been if it had remained a conversation just between the two of us. The students in our first Aesthetics of Atheism class at Fuller Seminary helped us identify promising avenues to pursue and, perhaps more importantly, those to avoid. In addition, the collection of friends and associates who offered guest lectures in that class also contributed substantively to our thoughts on the topic. So along with our students, we'd like to thank Peter Rollins, Tad DeLay, and Mike McHargue.

Others read early drafts of the manuscript and provided insightful feedback not only about the claims we were making, but also about how clearly we were—or more accurately, were not—communicating those claims. Joshua Beckett was the first to read a complete draft of the manuscript (even if out of order), and his critical commentary proved invaluable.

Joshua Jalandoon and Sooho Lee were helpful interlocutors in this regard as well, and so too was Tamisha Tyler, who has been an ongoing partner in helping us broaden the primary sources from which we draw. Sarah Schnitker, Madison Kawakami Gilbertson, Robert K. Johnston, Oliver Crisp, and Tommy Givens either read and responded to early drafts or listened patiently to us ramble incoherently about our project. We owe each of these individuals a debt of gratitude.

We also want to thank our editor, Emily Brower, who helped us turn a potentially inaccessible manuscript into something that was not merely provocative but readable, too. Her belief in the broader appeal of our book and its central idea is what drove her to spend far more time poring over our work than she would have otherwise. We are grateful for her editorial direction and her vote of confidence.

Barry would like to thank the Radical Theology reading group—particularly Ken, Chris, Sam, and Simon—that met for so many years as we slogged our way through challenging texts to find new language for theology after the death of god. And I offer thanks to my amazing music-making companions and the rest of the Sunday crowd for so often making life much brighter, and to Oliver Muirhead and Pete Rollins for coffees and countless hours of talking about everything but theology at Deus Ex Machina. Finally, thank you to Maria, whose smile broke open my world and who gives me more than I could ever return.

Kutter would like to thank my wife, Jessica, and my three daughters, Callie, Mattie, and Maeve. Along with the family members of so many authors, they know full well that "of the making of many books, there is no end" (Eccl 12:12). I cannot thank them enough for giving their dad and husband the space and time to commit to a seemingly endless task, the final product of which is a mere drop in what may very well be an ocean of meaninglessness. I couldn't do any of this without them.

Introduction

Certain elements of the story may be somewhat apocryphal. But what isn't in question is that Ernest Rutherford's gold leaf experiment radically shifted humanity's understanding of material reality. Rutherford, known by some as the father of nuclear physics, designed an experiment in which he sent alpha particles through a few pieces of gold leaf. The results confirmed that, just as others had hypothesized, atoms (and therefore all physical objects) indeed comprise mostly empty space. Legend has it that the following morning, Rutherford woke up and swung his feet over the side of his bed as he always did. But on this particular day, he found himself paralyzed with fear. He could not bring himself to set his feet upon the ground because he was convinced that he would simply fall through the floor.

The image of Rutherford dangling his legs over the side of his bed, staring down at what he understood to be an infinite abyss of empty space beneath him, offers a kind of living metaphor for the existential state in which many contemporary people find themselves. Not everyone may articulate it in precisely this way, but it is increasingly the case that many feel deep within their lived experience a certain kind of angst and anxiety, driven by the fact that they can no longer trust the ground beneath their feet to hold them up. Their awareness of how the world is structured has so fundamentally shifted that, when it comes to pressing questions about belief and un- or nonbelief, theism and atheism, it's as if they are sitting on their beds, feet hanging over the edge, and all they can see is a vast and empty expanse.

For those who find themselves in this somewhat precarious position, there seem to be two basic options. One possibility is to tell a story that simply rejects as a matter of fact this new way of understanding the world. In this telling, an increasingly secular society is fundamentally at odds with theism in general and Christianity in particular. And the only appropriate response—that is, the only "faithful" response—is to return to that glorious ur-time when people had better things to do than shoot particles through gold leaf.

A second possibility would be to tell a very different kind of story—one in which floors never really existed. In this telling, those who believe in such things either are products of the ignorance and superstitions that defined pre-Enlightenment society or are knowingly closing their eyes and shutting their ears to the evidence before them. Either way, because modern people have grown out of these "immature" and "unenlightened" notions, religious faith and theistic belief are only for those who either lack the courage to face reality or simply refuse to grow up.[1] Theism is a weakness and a scourge, an "opiate for the masses" that numbs the pain of the oppressed and assuages the guilt of the oppressor.

A distinct kind of late-modern anxiety sustains these divergent narratives, both of which have their fair share of champions and detractors. If the loudest voices are to be trusted, a choice simply must be made. Nothing short of absolute allegiance to one of these totalizing, mutually exclusive, explanatory frameworks will do. But when all is said and done, neither option is any more satisfying than the other, because neither helps anyone do what they actually need to do: get out of bed.

A/theism as Neither/Nor

One of the primary reasons for this kind of existential paralysis is that contemporary persons too often think about theism and atheism as if they were located at the opposite ends of a polarity, forever in conflict or in need of reconciliation (with Richard Dawkins on one end and David Bentley Hart on the other).[2] But it isn't just ardent atheists who operate as if the opposition between theism and atheism is self-evident. A number of prominent Christian thinkers also suggest that contemporary atheism—represented most fully by the new atheists like Dawkins and his associates Daniel Dennett, Sam Harris, and Christopher Hitchens—is inherently incompatible with any sort of theism, especially Christianity. According to the more vocal members of this camp, because modernity and its even more sinister sibling postmodernity are fundamentally at odds with any sort of theistic framework, the only appropriate response for the faithful is to cast off the wholly modern, presumably secular, view of the world they have inherited and instead adopt a premodern outlook more amenable to Christianity.[3] From this view, the choice is clear and simple: one must either reject atheism in favor of theism, or vice versa.

If only things were so straightforward and simple. In fact, there is a growing consensus among historians that modern secularity in the West—however it may be defined—has emerged not so much as a rejection of religion or theism, but rather as one of the many (unintended) consequences of the Protestant Reformations and their various intratribal religious conflicts.[4] And if this is indeed the case, atheism can no more cast off its religious heritage than theism can discard the very atheism that animates it.[5] Indeed, the two are intimately bound up with each other, so much so that new categories and terminology are needed in order to avoid what are otherwise misleading and unhelpful distinctions.[6]

Because the traditional language of atheism and theism is proving itself to be increasingly inadequate for the task at hand, the term a/theism serves as a helpful alternative.[7] The built-in ambiguity of this turn of phrase is intentional, for it leverages the richness of language. Indeed, just as philosopher John Gray suggests in his *Seven Types of Atheism*, "Rather than signifying equivocation or confusion, ambiguous expressions allow us to describe a fluid and paradoxical world."[8] Thus, a/theism is an ambiguous expression designed to function as a kind of heuristic device, signaling not the simple negation of theism (as with atheism), but instead an irreducibly complex, dynamic, and emergent mode of making meaning in a world where there might very well be no meaning at all.

Refusing to define atheism in a discrete or simplistic way generates the space necessary to capture—and make some sense of—the wide range of responses to life as it is lived in contemporary society. It also acknowledges the fact that, for most modern people, one's movement toward the atheistic side of the atheism-theism spectrum (or perhaps even beneath or beyond it) isn't perceived or experienced merely as a loss, but rather as an embrace of something constructive and, in many cases, life-giving.

In fact, rather than a failure on the part of non- or unbelievers, this a/theistic impulse actually reveals a lack or malfunction within the Christian imagination. It signals a yearning within the human person that is for one reason or another not satisfied by traditional religious expressions. As a consequence, the way forward cannot be a matter of choosing between either atheism or theism. But neither is it to bring together both theism and atheism in a way that generates some kind of magical synthesis between two otherwise mutually exclusive realities. Rather than either/or or both/and, to get out of bed and actually walk upon the empty space below, one must navigate a much more daunting reality: neither/nor.[9]

Christian A/theism

For believers and nonbelievers alike, neither atheism nor theism will do, but the need for a more robust a/theism that resists these reductive categories is especially pressing for all those who, despite their supposedly "secular" surroundings, continue to find themselves haunted by the perverse core of Christianity. In fact, when one listens closely to contemporary a/theism and takes seriously the aesthetic shape of its vision, a much deeper and more textured reality lying just beneath the surface of the rigid and artificial binary of belief-unbelief comes into view. To engage the world theologically, much less Christianly, one must go through the a/theistic experience.

At least that's what Jesus's cry on the cross would seem to suggest. Indeed, it is not incidental that Jesus chose to quote Psalm 22:1 with his dying breath: "My God, my God, why have you forsaken me?" (Matt 27:46; Mark 15:34). The Gospel accounts provide both the Greek (*egkataleipo*) and Aramaic (*sabachthani*) versions of his final words. The divine father, according to these texts, "forsakes" or "abandons" the son. But in the original Hebrew poem, the psalmist accuses God of something far more disturbing: apostasy (*'azab* means "to apostatize"). In this moment, an ontic rupture of epic proportions occurs; God apostatizes against God's very self.[10]

Whether religious or not, few want to follow this line of thought where it truly leads, and for good reason. It's too radical. It doesn't really matter if one's context is bourgeois or bohemian, post-liberal or alt-right. This kind of divine a/theism can only ever disrupt, unsettle, and disperse. Its critical edge cannot be softened. It cannot be domesticated, nor can it be co-opted, for no one possesses it. That's why G. K. Chesterton called Jesus's a/theistic cry "terribly revolutionary. . . . A matter more dark and awful than it is easy to discuss . . . a matter which the greatest saints and thinkers have justly feared to approach."[11]

Chesterton is sometimes guilty of hyperbole, but not in this case. Something is genuinely at stake here, especially for the Christian. The mere suggestion that there is "only one religion [i.e., Christianity] in which God seemed for an instant to be an atheist"[12] strikes many people of faith as not only "dark and awful," but downright heretical. It could be for this very reason that Chesterton—now a patron saint within many conservative Christian circles—strategically titled the book in which he makes God out to be an atheist *Orthodoxy*.

But just because something is unsettling doesn't mean it is heterodox. In fact, it is quite often the very opposite. Jürgen Moltmann, one of the most influential theologians in the twentieth century, made a similarly "dark and awful" move in his groundbreaking *The Crucified God*. According to Moltmann, even though it is often upsetting for Christians to hear Nietzsche's proclamation that "God is dead," God's abandonment of God on the cross is in fact the origin of the Christian faith.[13]

Needless to say, the further down this a/theistic rabbit hole one goes, the more any simple concept of "God," "theism," or "atheism" falls apart. To be sure, the allure of oversimplification will always persist, but contemporary a/theism resists such easy enticements. If anything, it moves in the opposite direction—toward rather than away from complexity. In so doing, it provides a unique lens by which to catch a glimpse, perhaps for the first time, of the scandalous heart of the Christian faith.[14]

The Aesthetics of A/theism

As interesting as these claims about a/theism and Christianity may be, they tell only part of the story. What is more, they aren't necessarily new. Others have already demonstrated some of the many ways in which a/theism provides a much-needed critical lens for understanding the Christian faith.[15] However, what is unique, and what may prove to be far more provocative, is the assertion that a/theism levels its critique in and through aesthetic means. To put a more positive spin on what is, in fact, the central thesis of this book, there is an (often unrecognized) aesthetic dimension to contemporary a/theism that, at its very core, is theologically significant.

To say that a/theism bears an aesthetic shape is to say that its formal characteristics are best understood in terms of aesthetics. Understanding the formal dimensions of a/theism in this way is to acknowledge not only that it is a fundamentally aesthetic project, but also that aesthetics illuminates important elements of contemporary a/theism that might otherwise go unnoticed. Chief among others is its willingness to draw upon the Christian tradition as a constructive resource for navigating the trauma of existence.

But for us to develop this central claim in any meaningful way, more needs to be said about what "aesthetics" means exactly, especially because, much like a/theism, this particular term tends to be a bit esoteric and is often used in ways that exclude the uninitiated rather than lead them toward deeper understanding. At its most basic, aesthetics is simply a philosophical discipline that deals with the nature, expression, and perception of beauty. The classical, philosophical approach to aesthetics, which locates its origins as far back as Plato (and possibly even Pythagoras), is largely concerned with the question of Beauty—a transcendent category existing in the realm of eternal forms that, along with Goodness and Truth, is wholly detached from the concrete world. Those who are interested more specifically in theological aesthetics share nearly identical conceptions of Beauty with this philosophical tradition. The primary exception is that theological aesthetics is additionally concerned with the ways in which Beauty bears some kind of relationship with the Divine.

However, from a more phenomenological perspective, aesthetics is the examination of sensory-emotional values. It is the exploration of feelings, tastes, and moods toward art, nature, and what might be called beauties (with a lowercase *b*)—affective experiences and sensual responses prompted by concrete forms of life. From this point of view, aesthetics considers the ways in which artists imagine, create, and perform works of art, as well as how people use, enjoy, and criticize art. It also concerns how art affects their moods, beliefs, and attitudes toward life.

Broadly speaking, then, aesthetics denotes a way of talking about humanity's basic awareness of reality—how fully embodied human beings see and feel and touch and taste the world around them. As cognitive scientists and philosophers of mind like Mark Johnson have suggested, this broader view of aesthetics is necessary for understanding the full depth and breadth of human meaning making, for just as there is no human meaning without aesthetics, there are no aesthetic categories that operate independently of the human body.[16]

Indeed, the Greek term *aisthetikos* simply means "sensitive" or "perceptive." It comes from the verb meaning "to perceive or to feel," a capacity that requires an apparatus capable of sensual perception, otherwise known as a body. It has to do with one's ability to perceive or feel the depth of reality as it confronts the human subject. It's what neuroscientist Antonio Damasio calls "the feeling of what happens"—a fully embodied, affective awareness of the world.[17] In other words, to invoke the aesthetic is to suggest that humans encounter in their concrete, embodied experiences an excess of meaning that resists logical reduction, and in the pages that follow, the term aesthetics will be used to signal this broader domain of embodied awareness and sensed perceptions.[18]

An aesthetics of a/theism is therefore an exploration of the dispositions and sentiments not only of the arts, but also of a society moving increasingly toward a post-theistic future, toward a world of new gods and new ideas. It names an attempt to capture the mood, the spirit of the times, through an exploration of particular pieces of art, specific artists, and the shifting dynamics of religion in the twenty-first century. In this way, an aesthetics of a/theism serves as both a site for theological exploration and an essential resource for articulating the Christian faith in a way that contemporary people might actually understand.

All this being said, a second, equally important thesis follows directly from the first claim that a/theism bears an aesthetic shape and that its principal critiques of Christianity (and theism in general) are aesthetic in nature. Namely, the aesthetic sensibilities of a/theism are embodied in material artifacts. What this means is that, in order to understand how a/theism functions in a post-secular world, one must first understand its concrete, cultural productions.

Popular culture is key in this regard, for pop-cultural forms like television and film map out the new terrain upon which post-secular life happens (i.e., they identify the "where"). Along similar lines, pop-cultural artifacts like popular music describe the primary trauma that has upended the world (i.e., they name the "what"). As a result, these cultural productions not only embody the aesthetics of a/theism, but also shed light on numerous dimensions of contemporary a/theism that might otherwise go overlooked or misunderstood. At the same time, the a/theistic vision that structures and shapes the contemporary cultural imagination sheds light on these cultural artifacts, offering a hermeneutical lens by which to analyze and interpret their power and meaning.

But material culture functions in another vital capacity as well. That is, it serves as a—if not the—primary resource for contemporary persons attempting to navigate a world still reeling from the death of god (i.e., it imagines the "how").

Anthony Pinn makes a similar suggestion in *The End of God-Talk*, in which he develops an "African American nontheistic humanist theology" by drawing upon ordinary cultural productions as the primary source material for his a/theological reflections.[19] Rather than the "sacred texts" of the Christian tradition, Pinn's nontheistic theology draws from African American literature, visual arts, music, architecture, and even momentarily dedicated spaces like barber shops, community centers, and one's local Starbucks.[20] Although Pinn approaches material culture with a series of theoretical concerns in mind, his focused exploration of the aesthetics of African American cultural productions underscores the numerous ways in which popular culture now functions as a vital resource for a world increasingly detached from the traditional categories of religion and theism. Indeed, the best of popular culture is able to serve in all three capacities—identifying the where, the what, and the how of contemporary life.

A third and final thesis, which assumes but doesn't automatically follow from the first two, is that the aesthetics of a/theism serves as an essential resource not only for navigating a post-secular world, but also for (re)reading the Christian tradition and its sacred texts. Along these lines, it will become increasingly clear that the aesthetic heart of contemporary a/theism does indeed offer a much-needed critique of Christianity (and every other theistic project, for that matter). But even this claim masks one that is much more radical: the

strong aesthetic vision that both animates and orients contemporary a/theism actually opens a kernel of Christianity
that is otherwise inaccessible. Indeed, more so than anything
else, it is the aesthetic shape of a/theism that provides it with
such profound religious insights. But it's also both more and
different than that. That is to say, the aesthetic vision of
a/theism actually creates the very conditions for faith—especially Christian faith.

The Death of the Death of God

At least in the modern West, theists in general and people of
Christian faith in particular have been grappling with these
a/theistic conditions for quite some time. After all, Nietzsche
pronounced the death of god in the late nineteenth century.
The same cannot be said of the Majority World (Asia, Africa,
and South America), which continues to experience a
rapid intensification and acceleration of faith and religion.[21]
These stark sociological differences between Western culture and the Majority World highlight the hyperlocal, con-
textually specific nature of any exploration of contemporary
a/theism. They also suggest that neither a/theism nor aesthetics as presently defined is in a position to make any kind of
universal claims about human life and meaning, for both are
decidedly Western phenomena.

At the same time, the very fact that Europe and North
America seem to be encountering a surge in a/theistic sensibilities during a time of global religious renewal is compelling in its own right, in large part because the very notion

that the West was ever truly "secular" or should now be considered "post-secular" is currently under reconsideration. As Gray suggests, whether it's the utopian dreams of transhumanists like Ray Kurzweil or political movements ranging from Ayn Rand's individualism to Marx's communism, the Western tradition of thought simply cannot help but produce ersatz religions. According to Gray, "The belief that we live in a secular age is an illusion. . . . With the revival of religion in recent times, we may seem to be living in a post-secular era. But since secular thinking was not much more than repressed religion, there never was a secular era."[22] Put differently, what Western culture is now encountering is neither increased secularity per se nor religious renewal, but more accurately, the sudden loss of a secular age that never was—the death of the death of god.

The death of the death of god thus defines the localized context in which the aesthetics of a/theism operates and flourishes. But to borrow a turn of phrase from Cornel West, the starting point for exploring this (mostly Western) phenomenon is not merely to acknowledge its unique "context." The starting point is rather the "catastrophic."[23] Some would describe this mode of doing theology as starting from the ground up, but that would be to understate the matter. It would also be to misunderstand the basic direction in which modern life unfurls. No one is going up. Instead, everyone is going down. Reality itself starts at ground zero—in the chaos of existence. It descends from there into the catastrophic.

On the Edge of the Abyss

Consider again the tale of Ernest Rutherford and the plunge into chaos that threatened his existence that fateful morning. At first blush, it appears as if he were limited to one of two options. Either he could ignore his newfound knowledge and step with naïve certainty upon the firm and stable ground beneath him, or he could remain forever in his bed, paralyzed by the sheer terror of a world without any kind of meaningful substance. In fact, though, another option was available to him. It's one that, admittedly, requires a bit more imagination to see. Rather than sit courageously on his bed or stand defiantly on the floor, Ernest Rutherford could have taken the more poetic route and danced on the edge of the abyss.[24]

If dancing seems like a counterintuitive response to an existential crisis of this or any other kind, that's because it is. But for those seeking to establish new coordinates in the wake of the death of the death of god, it may very well be the only way forward. It isn't about exerting one's will to power over a cold and meaningless universe. It's about giving meaning to form. For within the ever-emerging context of contemporary Western culture—one that is much like Rutherford's—the dawning of each day presents a new set of difficulties that were literally inconceivable just moments before. So much is changing at such increasingly rapid rates that, in certain important respects, change itself has changed. The religious landscape that was once imagined as timeless, fixed, and permanent has undergone a radical upheaval. As a consequence, when it comes to explorations of belief and unbelief, theism and atheism, faith and doubt, the only thing of which anyone can be sure today is that the once-stable ground of certainty has given way and revealed a gaping chasm.

Needless to say, there's no going back to a time when things were more steady and sure. But it also won't do any good to stay in bed forever. So we might as well get up and dance.

Notes

1. This describes what Charles Taylor calls the "subtraction story" of modern secularity. Taylor is highly critical of this narrative, in large part because it is reductive and unhelpful. See Charles Taylor, *A Secular Age* (Cambridge, MA: Harvard University Press, 2007).

2. We could add any number of theologians, scientists, and philosophers who traffic in this kind of either/or binary. But Dawkins and Hart are representative of those who passionately defend one position over and against the other. See David Bentley Hart, *Atheist Delusions: The Christian Revolution and Its Fashionable Enemies* (New Haven: Yale University Press, 2010); and Richard Dawkins, *The God Delusion* (New York: Mariner, 2006).

3. Hans Boersma has suggested that the "Christian-Platonic synthesis" that existed prior to the Enlightenment is the ideal framework for Christian theology. Neither modern rationalism nor postmodern irrationalism or antirealism is compatible with a truly Christian vision. See Hans Boersma, *Heavenly Participation: The Weaving of a Sacramental Tapestry* (Grand Rapids: Eerdmans, 2011). A strikingly similar move can be seen in the Radical Orthodoxy movement, e.g., Tracy Rowland, *Culture and the Thomist Tradition: After Vatican II* (New York: Routledge, 2003).

4. Among others, Brad S. Gregory and Michael Buckley both suggest that modern atheism is a direct consequence of the theological conflicts and explorations that were sparked by the Protestant

Reformation. See Brad S. Gregory, *The Unintended Reformation: How a Religious Revolution Secularized Society* (Cambridge, MA: Harvard University Press, 2012); and Michael J. Buckley, *Denying and Disclosing God: The Ambiguous Progress of Modern Atheism* (New Haven: Yale University Press, 2004). Coming from a somewhat different angle, Charles Taylor outlines three different forms of "secularity" in his magisterial *A Secular Age*, the third of which represents his preferred take on belief and unbelief in the modern world. For Taylor, all "believers" exist in a world where their core narratives are but one of numerous other options and are thus contested and conflicted. Likewise, though, all "doubters" are "haunted" by the specter of transcendence and therefore cannot entirely escape the longing for "fullness" that a wholly immanent frame cannot supply. See Charles Taylor, *A Secular Age* (Cambridge, MA: Harvard University Press, 2007).

5. Approaching the topic as an atheist and public intellectual, John Gray makes a compelling case for the interdependence of atheism and theism in John Gray, *Seven Types of Atheism* (New York: Penguin Random House, 2018).

6. Readers who are concerned with the biblical data regarding theistic "belief" might point to Rom 1:20–23 NET (New English Translation) as evidence of a binary view of theism and atheism—the very conceptualization we are rejecting: "For since the creation of the world his invisible attributes—his eternal power and divine nature—have been clearly seen, because they are understood through what has been made. So people are without excuse. For although they knew God, they did not glorify him as God or give him thanks, but they became futile in their thoughts and their senseless hearts were darkened. Although they claimed to be wise, they became fools and exchanged the glory of the immortal God for an image resembling mortal human beings or birds or four-footed animals or reptiles." Two things can be said here. First, without denying Paul's exhortation to the Romans, we are addressing a new and, thus, different situation. First-century Rome simply is not the twenty-first-century West. Second, we take as our a/theological starting point the second chapter of Romans, in which Paul goes on to state, "For it is not those who hear the law who are righteous before God, but those who do the law will be declared righteous. For whenever the Gentiles, who do not have the law, do by nature the things required by the law, these who do not have the law are a law to themselves. They show that the work of the law is written in

their hearts, as their conscience bears witness and their conflicting thoughts accuse or else defend them, on the day when God will judge the secrets of human hearts, according to my gospel through Christ Jesus" (Rom 2:13–16 NET). In our engagement with a/theism, we have in mind the "righteous Gentiles" who may very well deny God, but who nonetheless exhibit a faithfulness to the law "written on their hearts," which, according to Paul, is capable of "defending them" on the final day of judgment. The resonance between Paul's thought and Simon Critchley's notion of the "faith of the faithless" is evident, which is why our claims regarding a/theism are nowhere near as scandalous as the apostle Paul's.

7. We are borrowing this locution from Mark C. Taylor, *Erring: A Postmodern A/theology* (Chicago: University of Chicago Press, 1984).

8. Gray, *Seven Types of Atheism*, 6–7. Calvin Warren makes a similar claim about the fruitful ambiguity of visual images in Calvin L. Warren, *Ontological Terror: Blackness, Nihilism, and Emancipation* (Durham, NC: Duke University Press, 2018).

9. We will return to the notion of "neither/nor" in a later chapter, but as we consider how this pairing helps us articulate the aesthetics of a/theism, it should be noted that we are borrowing substantially from the work of Mark C. Taylor, *After God* (Chicago: University of Chicago Press, 2007).

10. "He passed in some superhuman manner through our human horror of pessimism. When the world shook and the sun was wiped out of heaven, it was not at the crucifixion, but at the cry from the cross: the cry which confessed that God was forsaken of God. And now let the revolutionists choose a creed from all the creeds and a god from all the gods of the world. . . . They will not find another god who has himself been in revolt. . . . They will find only one divinity who uttered their isolation; only one religion in which God seemed for an instant to be an atheist." G. K. Chesterton, *Orthodoxy* (Chicago: Moody Publishers, 2009), 162.

11. Chesterton, *Orthodoxy*, 161.

12. Chesterton, *Orthodoxy*, 162.

13. "A radical theology of the cross cannot give any theistic answer to the question of the dying Christ. Were it to do so it would evacuate the cross. Nor can it give an atheistic answer. Were it to do so it would no longer be taking Jesus' dying cry to God seriously. The

God of theism cannot have abandoned him, and in his forsakenness he cannot have cried out to a non-existent God. . . . Crude atheism for which this world is everything is as superficial as the theism which claims to prove the existence of God from the reality of this world." Jürgen Moltmann, *The Crucified God: The Cross of Christ as the Foundation and Criticism of Christian Theology*, trans. R. A. Wilson and John Bowden (Minneapolis: Fortress Press, 1993), 225–26. It is not for nothing that, in the eyes of many, Moltmann is no less of a heretic than Origen.

14. The philosopher Slavoj Žižek—himself a thoroughgoing materialist—has given a name to this unsettling reality. What Chesterton called "revolutionary," and Moltmann identified as "atheism for God's sake," Žižek calls the "perverse core" of the Christian faith—the divine a/theism that constitutes the incarnation qua incarnation. For Žižek, it is this unrecognized kernel of Christianity that provides him with an unparalleled resource for his critique of all ideologies. Indeed, it is the Christian tradition in particular that grounds Žižek's ethical and political project: "My claim here is not merely that I am a materialist through and through, and that the subversive core of Christianity is accessible also to a materialist approach; my thesis is much stronger: this kernel is accessible only to a materialist approach—and vice versa: to become a true dialectical materialist, one should go through the Christian experience." Slavoj Žižek, *The Puppet and the Dwarf: The Perverse Core of Christianity* (Cambridge, MA: MIT Press, 2003), 6.

15. In this regard, we are of course building on the work of those who have come before us. Nearly three decades ago, Merold Westphal's *Suspicion and Faith* offered an illuminating take on the religious uses of modern atheism. From Westphal's view, the atheism of Freud, Marx, and Nietzsche presents religious communities with a much-needed critique concerning the self-serving functions of religious practices and belief. Rather than conceive of atheism as the enemy or antithesis of religion, Westphal approaches atheism in terms of its prophetic role. By calling out humanity's seemingly infinite capacity for self-deception (Freud), the idolatrous substance of any and all "faiths" (Marx), and the religiously codified moralism that conceals self-interested behavior (Nietzsche), modern atheists are (perhaps unknowingly) plagiarizing the very same critiques uttered by Amos, Jeremiah, and Isaiah to the people of God. And just as it was with these prophetic forebears, says Westphal, religious persons refuse to listen to modern atheists at their own peril. We

are assuming a similar kind of posture to Westphal's, but we want to take his argument one step—or maybe even numerous steps—further. See Merold Westphal, *Suspicion and Faith: The Religious Uses of Modern Atheism* (Grand Rapids: Eerdmans, 1993).

16. See Mark Johnson, *The Meaning of the Body: Aesthetics of Human Understanding* (Chicago: University of Chicago Press, 2007).

17. See Antonio Damasio, *The Feeling of What Happens: Body and Emotion in the Making of Consciousness* (Boston: Mariner, 2000).

18. In many respects, we are adopting a similar approach to Alain de Botton in his *Art as Therapy* and *Religion for Atheists*. In fact, if not for an abiding fear of being labeled derivative, we could have easily titled our book *A/theism for Theists*. We even have a slightly overlapping, although clearly distinct, audience. But unlike de Botton, we're not trying to rescue or reclaim anything, religious or otherwise. Instead, as we move from one chapter to the next and consider various manifestations of contemporary art, our goal will be to name what often goes unnamed: the strong aesthetic vision of atheism in both art and philosophy. See Alain de Botton, *Religion for Atheists: A Non-Believer's Guide to the Uses of Religion* (New York: Pantheon, 2012). See also Alain de Botton and John Armstrong, *Art as Therapy* (London: Phaidon, 2016).

19. Anthony B. Pinn, *The End of God-Talk: An African American Humanist Theology* (New York: Oxford University Press, 2012).

20. Pinn, *The End of God-Talk*, 22.

21. We are thankful to Joshua Beckett for reminding us of the need to locate this exploration of a/theism in a decidedly Western context. Much more work needs to be done concerning the oddity that is Western "secularity" in the midst of an increasingly religious global population.

22. Gray, *Seven Types of Atheism*, 72.

23. West invoked the "catastrophic" in a dialogue with prominent atheist Simon Critchley, author of *Faith of the Faithless*. Simon Critchley and Cornel West, "The Faith of the Faithless," BAM, February 7, 2012, available on YouTube at https://tinyurl.com/ybjrdzc7. In other public comments, West has expanded on how this posture generates a healthy approach to atheism: "A certain kind of atheism is always healthy . . . because what atheism does, it at least cleans the deck because it claims that all gods are idols. And most gods are idols. It's just that the prophetic traditions, be

it Judaism, Islam, or Christianity, are tied to this God of love and justice. . . . So a lot of folk who've lost faith in god, it's a very healthy thing because the god that they've lost faith in was probably an idol anyway." See "Cornel West on a Healthy Atheism," Union Theological Seminary, October 6, 2014, available on YouTube at https://tinyurl.com/nmpczne.

24. "One could imagine a delight and a power of self-determining, and a freedom of will, whereby a spirit could bid farewell to every belief, to every wish for certainty, accustomed as it would be to support itself on slender cords and possibilities, and to dance even on the verge of abysses." Friedrich Nietzsche, *The Gay Science (The Joyful Wisdom)*, trans. Thomas Common (Digireads.com, 2009), 135.

PART I

The Where

1

A Genre: Horror

Human beings love to tell stories about the basic unknow-
able-ness that conditions everything—ethereal stories about
ghosts and monsters and the undead (or reanimated), stories
where the world that exists encounters a world that does not.
Often, these stories evoke visceral responses, for they play
upon the listener's fears, dreads, and anxieties. At times, they
are downright horrifying, which is why they are called "horror stories." Nevertheless, these stories have long served as
one of the primary means by which individuals and communities seek to name, know, and even interact with that which
perpetually haunts them, that which is somehow present to
them even—and perhaps especially—in its absence.

Late-modern society is experiencing a moment of renewed
fascination with the pervading sense of ghostliness these horror stories contain. It's a ghostliness rooted in negation—a
catastrophic absence that includes both the trauma of past
losses and the terrifying prospect of a future that is now

lost, too, or at least receding.[1] Think of the 2017 movie *Get Out*, a story that generates horror not through jump scares or other generic conventions, but through a taut exploration of a uniquely devastating trauma (i.e., racism) that not only haunts the narrative's present but also robs it of a future. As this Oscar-winning film demonstrates, the narrative worlds of contemporary horror are haunted not by a something or someone per se, but rather by an absent center—a no-thing and no-one.

While some may believe and even argue that present-day technocratic society has matured beyond the quaint superstitions of its pre-Enlightenment forebears, contemporary cultural productions suggest otherwise. Indeed, it would seem that no amount of scientific fideism or technological optimism has been able to fully exorcise the specter that hovers around the edges (and sometimes in the very center) of life as it is lived today. It may even be that the collective ignorance concerning the very scientific and technological advances upon which contemporary people so thoroughly depend has created the conditions for a return of the mysterious and the mystical.[2] For all its sophistication and enlightened rationality, the modern world remains haunted by a *je ne sais quoi*—a certain "we know not what." From this view, it would be a gross mischaracterization to conceive of the early decades of the twenty-first century as some kind of an extension or amplification of the glorious Age of Enlightenment. Far more fitting would be to understand this particular moment in time as the dawn of a new Dark Age. Or to put a finer point on the matter, dusk has arrived in the Age of Uncertainty.

Horror speaks from within this context. And when it does, the genre directly addresses the all-pervading uncertainty that currently haunts the cultural imagination. For the most part, it's a particular kind or subgenre of horror that functions in this way, which is why much has rightly been made of what might be called "supernatural" or "paranormal" horror. From literature like Bram Stoker's *Dracula*, to films like *Rosemary's Baby* and *The Exorcist*, and even to contemporary young-adult fiction like R. L. Stine's Goosebumps series, certain manifestations of the horror genre are concerned with the relationship between the natural world and its supernatural counterpart, generally making clear the (moral, philosophical, and theological) demarcations between the two.[3]

But there is another strain of horror that quite intentionally turns these metaphysical assumptions on their head—one that not only appropriates or inverts religious symbolism, but also often rejects the transcendent outright. It's a form of the genre that is notably a/theistic, which is not to say that it is antireligious or even reductively materialist, although it can be both. Rather, it's to say that, much like the work of horror writer H. P. Lovecraft (who was himself a staunch atheist), contemporary horror stories often unfold in a context in which God, the Divine, and the Super-natural are nowhere to be found. Yet, even here, the genre tends to belie stark atheism, instead hinting at what can only be called a religious or spiritual sensibility in the midst of this divine absence.[4]

This seeming paradox captures well the basic a/theistic impulse that gives shape to the formal elements of horror (and vice versa), but it's an impulse that typically goes unidentified or unrecognized as such, in part because it is embodied in particular instances of the genre, each of which reveals a unique dimension of the relationship between aesthetics and a/theism. As a consequence, to articulate the theological significance of a concrete cultural artifact of this kind—one in which the divine is utterly absent—requires a radical reordering of one's imagination. It involves reading horror as a kind of folk a/theology. In truth, the genre invites this kind of approach. In fact, it would seem that most horror fiction would have it no other way.

The Netflix series *Stranger Things* offers an illuminating example of how horror can serve as an a/theology of this sort, representing, as it does, one of the more current manifestations of the horror genre. It is also the case that its platform (an online streaming service), its distribution network (Netflix), and the consumption practices it generates (binge-watching) are as much a part of its aesthetic as the narrative content itself.[5] In other words, the unique modes by which people engage horror stories are part of the equation, too, and this series in particular highlights the shifting dynamics between consumers, producers, and the digitally mediated content they co-create.[6] Perhaps most importantly though, *Stranger Things* offers what is possibly one of the best encapsulations of the contemporary cultural imagination in recent memory, for it presents viewers with a resonant depiction of the location—the "where"—in which contemporary life now unfolds. In part because it operates according to the conventions of the horror genre, the show is able to place its audience in a context defined not by the natural or the supernatural, the human or the superhuman, but by the unhuman—a world haunted by the Upside Down.

The Haunting

Stranger Things makes no attempt to tell a universal story. Rather, it tells an incredibly local story firmly situated in a concrete time and place. In so doing, the series not only locates its characters in space and time. It also locates the viewer in a historically situated context that serves as the background conditions against which the entire narrative takes place.

Because *Stranger Things* simply assumes these background conditions as a matter of fact, it helps to make explicit a few key features of the show's (and by extension, the audience's) historically situated context, which philosopher and cultural theorist Charles Taylor has described as a "secular age."[7] Taylor points out that, not too long ago (say, five hundred years), the default assumption for most human beings was that the world was fundamentally "porous"—constantly open (and thus vulnerable) to a host of spirits, forces, and gods that not only transcended the material world, but actively impinged upon it. This, of course, is no longer the case. Indeed, the background conditions of belief have changed quite radically for contemporary people. Along with the advent of modernity came the rise of what Taylor calls the "buffered self," which conceives of both the individual human person and reality as a whole as closed off from transcendence. While it is certainly true that individuals continue to exhibit various degrees of "closed" or "open" takes on the nature of reality, many, if not most, people (whether religious or not) now live their lives within a closed world system.

It's not just that people today struggle to believe in God or the gods of a particular religion (Christian or otherwise). It's rather that the default position—the shared starting point—is one in which there is nothing "out there" to believe in at all. In telling the story about how Western society got to this point, Taylor suggests that the huge shifts involved in moving from a world where spirits and forces impinged upon daily life to a world where there is nothing more than what can be tasted and seen and touched have changed both how people doubt and how people believe. On the one hand, those who need no higher (i.e., transcendent) realm to make their life meaningful cannot seem to shake the ghosts of a once-porous world. They sense society's loss of belief as if it were a haunting presence, and as a result, they experience profound longings for a fullness or depth or meaning they once knew but have long since forgotten. On the other hand, those who do believe are equally haunted by doubt.

The basic assumption that there is no "out there" in the first place calls into question what it means to believe in a god, much less the God of a particular religious tradition. In this context, belief is neither easy nor given, but always already includes a pervasive sense of doubt. In other words, life in late modernity is fundamentally conflicted. It is "cross-pressured," to use Taylor's language. Every believer is uncertain, and every skeptic is haunted. More than anything else, it is this sense of hauntedness—the nontranscendent kind—that serves as the invisible but ever-present background in *Stranger Things*.

The Presence of an Absence

Like the secular age Taylor describes, the entire narrative world of *Stranger Things* is haunted, but not by the terrifying creature abducting humans in the dead of night. Nor is it haunted in the sense that some supernatural, disembodied agent is making its presence known in the natural realm. Rather, *Stranger Things* depicts a wholly immanent world haunted by vestiges of a transcendence that once was but no longer is. Case in point: the very first scene in the pilot episode provides viewers with a specific date. It's November 6, 1983. Something is amiss at the US Department of Energy's National Laboratory in Hawkins, Indiana. Inside, a scientist in a lab coat flees—from something. Viewers never see what is pursuing him, but the sound of atonal clusters and shrieking stinger chords gives a pretty good sense of what's about to happen. Needless to say, it doesn't end well for him.

Smash cut to a basement where a group of young boys are in the midst of a thirteen-hour Dungeons & Dragons campaign. Mike Wheeler, the dungeon master, offers play-by-play narration, while Dustin Henderson and Lucas Sinclair argue over competing strategies for defeating the dreaded Demogorgon who has just happened upon them. The fateful roll of the dice comes at the hands of Will Byers, the young man whose mysterious disappearance provides the impetus for the entire story. Will accidentally rolls the dice off the table, and as the boys scramble to discover the outcome of their heroic campaign, Mike's mother brings it unceremoniously to an end with her call to the dinner table. As Mike's three friends gather their bikes to ride home, Will confesses the truth: "The Demogorgon—it got me." His words soon prove prophetic, but they should come as no surprise. After all, the title of the first episode is "The Vanishing of Will Byers." As he rides into the night, that's exactly what transpires.

The remainder of season 1 is about Mike, Lucas, and Dustin's quest to rescue their missing friend Will. Along the way, they befriend a young girl named Eleven, whose scientifically engineered telekinetic powers provide them with the means not only to find Will, but also to defeat the creature that absconded with him in the first place. It's not entirely clear how much time (if any) passes between the scientist's death, Will's disappearance, and the beginning of their journey, but from a number of subtle and not-so-subtle hints scattered throughout the series, it would seem that all of the narrative events unfold during what is colloquially known as the holiday season. For instance, the intertitle in the final scene announces that the denouement occurs one month after the story's climax. In addition, given the non-diegetic music playing during this sequence ("Carol of the Bells" and "White Christmas"), the gift that Nancy (Mike's sister) gives to Jonathan (Will's brother), and the various decorations in and around their homes, it appears to be Christmas Eve, which would have been exactly one month after Thanksgiving Day in 1983 (Thanksgiving was on November 24 that year).[8] In other words, the entire story takes place between the days just before Thanksgiving and leading up to Christmas.

One of the more explicit references to the holiday season occurs in episode 3, which is titled "Holly Jolly." Joyce Byers (Will's mom) discovers that, by nailing Christmas lights to the walls of her house, she is able to communicate with her missing son. Interestingly enough, she is the only character in the show who mentions Christmas explicitly, claiming that she put up the lights because "Will always loved Christmas." Otherwise, no one utters a word about this or any other holiday. Instead, like the sporadically blinking lights that hover over the Byerses' home, these holy days function as the silent but ever-present backdrop for the horror that eventually unfurls. In a very literal sense, then, even though none of the characters acknowledges it or is perhaps even aware of it, traces of a once-religious past haunt every frame, conditioning what is otherwise a wholly immanent world.[9]

Religion isn't the only vestige of a bygone era pervading the world of *Stranger Things*. Along with religion, every other traditional institution seems to have collapsed as well. Even if they are not entirely defunct, they are, in practice, not to be trusted. This basic suspicion of institutions starts with the nuclear family, but it eventually expands to include industry, government, and education as well. The two central families in *Stranger Things*, the Byerses and the Wheelers, are foils for each other. Although the Wheeler nucleus remains intact, the father is detached, dismissive, and wholly unaware of how asinine his self-interested remarks actually are. He and his wife may still be married, but he is no more meaningfully involved in his children's lives than Lonnie Byers, the deadbeat father who returns only when his son is thought to be dead and he angles to collect money from a lawsuit.

As a result, neither the institutional structures of marriage nor parents themselves (fathers in particular) prove to be of much value to the young people who are trying to survive the trauma and chaos that surrounds them. But it's not simply that parents aren't invested in their children's lives. The deeper problem is that they actively betray their children's trust. The chief example of this betrayal is the ease with which the parents in *Stranger Things* align their interests with those of the all-seeing surveillance state. Rationalized in terms of protecting their helpless and innocent offspring (e.g., in episode 7), Karen and Ted Wheeler willingly hand their parental power over to an institutional monster that is as formidable as it is obscure: the government.

The tangible representative for this otherwise-faceless institution is Dr. Martin Brenner, who is the head of the Hawkins Laboratory. It comes as no surprise that his character turns out to be as terrifying as the flesh-eating creature he brings into the world, for his goal is not to defeat or even defend against it, but to translate its raw power into an instrument of terror. An even more horrifying aspect of Brenner's character is how he conceives of the young girl known simply as Eleven. To him, Eleven is not a human being but first and foremost a piece of technology. Although the mechanics of it all are not entirely clear, numerous flashbacks and dream sequences eventually reveal that Dr. Brenner not only has cultivated Eleven's psychic powers but has weaponized them as well. He trains her to enter the Upside Down (the parallel world where the creature resides) to surveil his enemies, to manipulate physical objects with her mind, and eventually to kill. Thus, while Eleven is clearly the innocent victim of his unyielding will to power, the end result is that she too is now a weapon of mass destruction—a monstrous figure begat by a monstrosity.

In this way, Dr. Brenner serves as the harbinger for another kind of all-encompassing power (the military-industrial complex) that haunts the narrative but isn't ever fully realized because it is always yet to come. It is a presence that is notably absent, exerting an influence upon the story world even while going unseen and unsaid. As the series progresses, it becomes clear that Brenner is a scientist operating under the auspices of the US military, but he is first and foremost an industrialist whose sole interest is the development of weapons technology. As such, Brenner embodies a much larger force that never explicitly appears in the narrative but nevertheless enables everything he does—namely, the government's co-opting of scientific and technological advancement under the pretense of "national security."

Whether it's a group of preteens fighting off Demogorgons or adult viewers staring into their digital media devices, no one contends with the specter of an all-seeing government, a fossilized religion, or even one's dysfunctional family without the proper resources. From the perspective of *Stranger Things*, the best resources for this kind of endeavor are found in popular culture, more specifically, popular culture from the 1980s. To say that *Stranger Things* is preoccupied with eighties pop culture would be an understatement. Every sight, sound, and structural element of the series—its entire formal aesthetic—is indebted to popular youth culture circa 1983. From role-playing games (Dungeons & Dragons), to music (the Clash), to food (Eggo waffles), to movies (*Star Wars*), to yes, even horror authors (Stephen King), *Stranger Things* plays as a kind of self-referential homage to an age in American society that was standing on the cusp of the digital revolution—a time when kids really could get lost in the woods or not know how to make a sensory deprivation tub without calling their science teacher at home on the weekend because they didn't carry sophisticated GPS units–cameras-flashlights-telephones-computers in their pockets.

In certain respects, *Stranger Things* evinces a kind of pre-digital naïveté that is as romanticized as it is real. But the aesthetic impulse of the show has to do with far more than a quick and easy nostalgia, even if that is part of the fun. Rather, in a context where all the traditional meaning-making structures—the institutions that once provided the necessary resources for making sense of life and the world (i.e., religion, family, politics)—have collapsed, popular culture is the only thing that still works. It is the de facto theology, philosophy, and political theory of contemporary culture. It functions as the shared meaning-making system that structures underlying myths and gives voice to future hopes. In other words, there is a reason that Dustin's repeated references to the Lando Calrissian betrayal in *The Empire Strikes Back* don't strike contemporary audiences as dated or mere nostalgia. It's not just because Disney has committed to continue the *Star Wars* franchise ad infinitum (although that surely has something to do with it). It's because this popular sci-fi franchise serves as part of the mythic substrate of contemporary society. Pop culture simply is the symbolic well from which many if not most people draw, regardless of when they were born or whether they've ever attended an eighties-themed party. What is more, it has emerged as an essential resource for navigating a context haunted by the ghosts of a once-religious world and a silent but increasingly deadly superstructure from which there is no escape.

The Catastrophic

Like visual bookends, the establishing shots for the pilot episode of *Stranger Things* and the season 1 finale are identical. The first thing that comes into view is the night sky. The camera then redirects the viewer's gaze, shifting from the starry expanses above to the ground below. It is a movement that not only signals the trajectory of the narrative (i.e., downward), but also focuses on the concrete site where all of the horror ostensibly originates: the US Department of Energy's Hawkins National Laboratory. Of course, it soon becomes clear that all sorts of monstrosities lurk beyond these walls, but this particular location stands out. It is the site where Dr. Brenner performs his experiments on Eleven. It also houses the primary portal to the Upside Down, which allows both the creature and humans to traverse what was once an impermeable boundary. In other words, it is the site of the catastrophic—literally an overturning (from the Greek *kata–strophe* to "overturn"). Within these walls is a deep and abiding trauma that has upended the world along with everything in it. As the downward movement of the camera intimates, this site is where the descent into chaotic darkness begins.

Significantly, the catastrophic dimension of the narrative is not isolated to the Hawkins Lab. Indeed, in a very real sense, the entire story world of *Stranger Things* is rooted in catastrophe. Whether it's Sheriff Hopper grappling with the death of his young daughter, or Joyce Byers dealing with the horror of a missing child, or Eleven navigating a world filled with adults she can no longer trust, everyone, it would seem, is trying to eke out an existence in light of some prior trauma.

Thus, much like the viewing audience that continues to reel from the death of god, these characters have also been thrown into a post-traumatic scenario. The particular way in which the characters respond to their concrete circumstances says something important about the nature of their beliefs and the aesthetic dimensions of this otherwise a/theistic world. In short, *Stranger Things* charts a shift in the contemporary cultural imagination from belief to hermeneutics—that is, from a concern about rational justifications for accepting the truth of a proposition (i.e., a belief) to the recognition that no one has direct access to "the facts," whatever they may be. Instead, everything is always already interpreted (i.e., hermeneutics).[10] From this point of view, it doesn't matter whether or not there is something objectively true out there to be known, for no one can see beyond their own horizon of understanding. There simply is no such thing as an unfiltered take on reality.

Although subtle, the title sequence of *Stranger Things* offers a visual representation of this epistemological move. In each and every episode, the opening credits conclude with on-screen text identifying the title of that particular installment. The words then move toward the foreground until they eventually swallow the camera whole. The result is that viewers enter the narrative world by literally going through the text, which means that, according to the terms established by the formal aesthetics of the series, there is no view from nowhere by which one might access or understand this narrative world. Everything anyone claims to "know" about the world and life in it is interpreted and interpretive—period. In other words, it's hermeneutics all the way down.

This, of course, isn't to deny that something above or beyond the narrative world might exist. After all, the stars really are out there, in the sky above. Rather, much like the descending movement of the camera, a shift in focus from belief to hermeneutics involves the redirection of one's gaze toward the concrete, the immanent, and the material. Hermeneutics is about interpreting what is given in concrete human experience, rather than searching for abstract, universal concepts to invest the world with meaning. It also implies that conversations about the kind of evidence (or lack thereof) that would warrant belief in a transcendent realm simply have no bearing on the core trauma that haunts existence. This sort of discourse is beyond merely irrelevant. It is nonsensical.

All told then, when this basic hermeneutical stance joins with an equally thoroughgoing distrust of traditional institutions, it becomes patently obvious that the cultural resources on offer simply no longer work. They don't speak to the trauma, chaos, and horror that constitute so much of lived experience. To start with, political institutions clearly aren't able to alleviate anyone's existential turmoil. If anything, they are part of the problem, which is why the government in *Stranger Things* so often functions as a cipher for a kind of absolute evil. But if politics has failed, neither reason (in the form of education and science) nor religion has done any better—a key point made explicit through various lines of dialogue. For example, in episode 5 ("The Flea and the Acrobat"), when the boys consult their earth and biology teacher, Mr. Clarke, about Carl Sagan's *Cosmos* and the possibility of accessing parallel universes, he reminds them, "Science is neat, but . . . it's not very forgiving." That is to say, science reveals a great deal about the nature of reality, but it has severe limitations, especially as it concerns the concrete fears and anxieties that plague most human beings.

Hopper echoes this same thought in the first episode when he and Mr. Clarke introduce themselves during the search for Will Byers. "I always had a distaste for science," says Hopper. "Sarah, my daughter—galaxies, the universe, whatnot—she always understood all that stuff. I always figured there was enough going on down here I never needed to look elsewhere." It is not incidental that, immediately after Hopper's soliloquy on the apparent worthlessness of science, an unnamed character reveals that Hopper's daughter had died tragically a few years before. His world has been overturned, and no amount of reason or scientific knowledge can undo that catastrophe. Nothing can make it right.

Much like Hopper, Joyce Byers faces a similar kind of traumatic scenario after paramedics pull a body thought to be Will Byers from a lake. Like any parent, she responds to the news of her child's death with disbelief and denial. But Joyce's rejection of the material "evidence" (i.e., Will's body) is more than the first stage of grief. It's a conclusion based upon a different kind of evidence altogether—a data set that is not empirically falsifiable. More specifically, her missing son is communicating with her through Christmas lights, and a faceless creature seems to be emerging out of the wall of her living room. She readily acknowledges to Hopper and to others that she knows it all "sounds crazy," but she remains steadfast in her conviction that her son is not dead. When her ex-husband Ronnie tells her "to seriously consider that all this—it's in your head," and she asks how then he might explain or otherwise make sense of the phenomena she has encountered, his advice is to "talk to a shrink, or to Pastor Charles." Her reply is as brief as it is telling, for it distills into three short words the show's basic take on the efficacy of reason, religion, and politics in addressing the traumatic loss of her child that haunts her every waking moment: "They can't help." Full stop.

The psychological sciences can't help because Joyce is not suffering from a mental break. Religion can't help because Will is not dead, so it can't be his "ghost" or some other supernatural "spirit" that is haunting her. And the government certainly can't help. They've created the whole mess. That's when Joyce stumbles upon a moment of genuine insight: "I know it sounds crazy. You think I don't know that? It *is* crazy."

Joyce's aha moment serves as a distillation of the context in which the show locates both its characters and the viewer. Time and again, the narrative of *Stranger Things* suggests in ways both explicit and implicit that the reference point for making sense of post-traumatic life is not the transcendent heavens above, but the catastrophic here and now. Given this on-the-ground reality, the audience, much like Joyce, is faced with one of two options. On the one hand, it may be that viewers need to muster the courage to admit that they really are crazy and that these phenomena are best explained in terms of psychological processes. Of course, that would be the easy answer. In that case, the remedy would simply be medicine or therapy or more time to grieve. On the other hand, these phenomena might not be the product of a delusional mind at all. They might even be real. And as Joyce points out, that truly is crazy.

The Monster(s)

As Joyce comes to realize, modern science and politics deny that anything haunts the world at all, while religion locates it in a realm entirely detached from concrete reality. But *Stranger Things* moves in an altogether different direction. It dares to suggest that a child actually has been abducted by a creature from another dimension and is now calling out for help. If this is indeed the case, the context in which life unfolds is far more horrific than anyone could have ever possibly imagined. Just ask Will Byers's friends. What *Stranger Things* imagines for its audience is a reality that is neither purely natural nor supernatural, neither strictly atheistic nor theistic, but haunted by the a/theistic presence of an absence. Enter the creature.

A particularly helpful way of conceptualizing the creature in *Stranger Things* is in terms of what French composer and critical theorist Michel Chion calls the *acousmêtre*.[11] The *acousmêtre* is a character with an ambiguous relationship to the screen because it is neither inside nor outside the image but is still wholly involved in the narrative, primarily through sound. Speaking in purely formal terms, the monster in *Stranger Things* is heard rather than seen. It makes its presence known through atonal musical clusters and dissonant sound effects rather than any visual cues in the frame. As such, it is quite literally the acoustic presence of a visual absence. Nevertheless, it is constantly lurking, implicated in the actions of the characters and the narrative world they navigate. The ambiguity between sound and image invests this heard-but-not-seen creature with a mysterious power that has become somewhat of a staple in the horror genre. Because it exists neither inside the image nor entirely outside the image, it operates in a realm that resists categorization or rationalization. Only when the monster receives full visual representation (at the end of episode 5) does the force it wields as the *acousmêtre* begin to recede.

Here, though, is where the creature in *Stranger Things* diverges in a key way from Chion's conceptualization. For Chion, the *acousmêtre* can be instantly dispossessed of its mysterious power when it is "*de-acousmatized*, when the film reveals the face that is the source of the voice."[12] When this occurs, what was once a nameless, faceless terror morphs into something more embodied, something more human. Chion's point is well taken. Human voices emerge from human faces, so to anchor a voice in a body is to humanize it. But this is precisely what the creature in *Stranger Things* is not—a human. Even though it does eventually receive full visual representation and is thus "de-acousmatized," the creature's face is never seen, not because the camera keeps it hidden from view, but because it doesn't have one. In fact, prior to the moment the audience sees the creature for the first time, numerous characters cite its lack of face as both its key feature and the very reason why they are unable to describe what "it" is with any kind of precision. Joyce comes closest when she says, "It was almost human, but it wasn't. It had long arms, and it didn't have a face."

Stranger Things leverages the dynamics of the sound–image relationship to complicate the human–monsters–unhuman relationship even further. The eventual unification of the creature's image with its sound reveals that it is neither merely human nor nonhuman, but is something altogether different: unhuman.[13] And it is this faceless, unhuman horror that now confronts characters and audience alike.

However, it is equally significant that, in the terms set forth by the narrative, this unhuman creature emerges as the unintended consequence of technological innovations developed by another faceless entity: the nation-state. The primary difference between the two is that the government is profoundly human, which means that its various machinations reveal the monstrous character of both human social arrangements and human beings themselves.

Eleven is a perfect example. Like Frankenstein's monster, she embodies all the horrors of a society's technophilia run amok (represented in each case by an individual man, Dr. Frankenstein and Dr. Brenner, respectively). Worse yet, she represents the co-opting of this technophilia by the military-industrial complex for its own self-interested ends. In other words, as innocent as she may appear, Eleven is a danger both to herself and to others. Her new friends seem to intuit this on some level, even if they don't fully understand its implications. Unlike the audience, they aren't privy to the title of episode 6, which just so happens to be "The Monster." But even with this extra-diegetic information, it isn't until the very end of the episode that the narrative identifies the specific character to which this title refers. Just as it is with many of the episodes in the first season of *Stranger Things*, "The Monster" ends with a cliffhanger, but in this case, it is literal. Mike has been forced to jump over a cliff to save Dustin from harm. Rather than falling to his potential death, Eleven saves him by suspending him in midair with her telekinetic powers. After rescuing Mike and just before the image fades to black, she baldly states what no one wants to admit: "I'm sorry, Mike. I opened the gate. I'm the monster."

To be sure, the unhuman creature that was once confined to the parallel world known as the Upside Down does indeed wreak havoc in the lives of these characters. But this violent intrusion is only made possible because a power-hungry scientist working on behalf of a power-obsessed government chooses to artificially boost a little girl's psychic powers through technological manipulation in order to open a passageway to the other side.

As it turns out, the truly monstrous element in *Stranger Things* is not the supposed monster at all. The faceless creature terrorizing Hawkins, Indiana, is merely an instance of the unhuman confronting the human. Is it terrifying? Absolutely. But a monster? Not so much. Indeed, the truly terrifying thought that *Stranger Things* presents is that maybe, just maybe, *humans* are the real monsters.

The Vale of Shadows

If humans are the real monsters in *Stranger Things* and the creature is "we know not what," then the realm from which this unknown something originates cannot be human either. It's why this parallel world is known simply as the Upside Down. As the show's aesthetic makes clear, popular culture provides the necessary resources that allow the characters to make some sense of this inexplicable but oh-so-real dimension. For instance, in episode 5, consulting what appears to be the *D&D Expert Rule Book*, Dustin reads, "The Vale of Shadows is a dimension that is a dark reflection, or echo, of our world. It is a place of decay and death, a plane out of phase, a [place] with monsters. It is right next to you, and you don't even see it."

Directly analogous to the Vale of Shadows, the Upside Down is a world that is most decidedly not for or about humans. It is wholly alien, not in the sense that it remains unexplored, but in the sense that it has nothing to do with humans at all. Indeed, it demonstrates an absolute lack of concern for their various comings and goings. If the *D&D Expert Rule Book* is a trustworthy guide, the Upside Down is like darkness itself, which surrounds a given space on every side but can never be seen, because it is the absence of that by which people do see (i.e., light). It's right next to the seeing agent, but it isn't visible. If this is indeed the logic by which it operates, then the inverse must also be true. That is, from the perspective of the Upside Down, humans are the ones who are invisible.

Stranger Things depicts the radical otherness of this world in a few ways, some of which are the stock and trade of the horror genre, others of which are less so. For example, the portals that open up to the Upside Down are dripping with ooze that covers what appear to be living roots or tentacles of some kind. Whatever in fact these slime-drenched branches are, far more important is the response they generate: disgust. For in the narrative world of *Stranger Things* (and the horror genre more broadly), the residual evidence of the encounter between the human and the unhuman worlds is as grotesque and repulsive as the encounter itself. Much like a human's gag reflex, the unhuman also rejects toxic, alien substances from its system with equal parts violence and spontaneity. And the by-product of this involuntary revulsion is never pretty. In fact, it's fairly revolting.

The toxicity runs in both directions. As Joyce and Hopper discover in the final episode when they enter the Upside Down to rescue Will, the air itself is toxic for humans to breathe. When they do eventually find him, he is on the verge of death, his body having been slowly consumed by the living structures of this "place of decay and death." Yet the fact that not only do they find Will's body, but he is also still alive (although just barely) serves as evidence that the Upside Down, although unsuitable for sustaining human life, is not any kind of otherworldly, disembodied plane of existence.

As Mike states clearly in response to Dustin's suggestion that Eleven might be channeling Will's ghost, "It's not his ghost. He's not dead. Will is alive!" In other words, *Stranger Things* is not a story about ghosts or the spirit realm or the afterlife. There's nothing supernatural about it. Rather, it is a story about the living, breathing, enfleshed body of a boy who is caught on the other side of a Vale, suspended in a world that was never meant for him. The Upside Down isn't "above" or "beyond" the natural world (i.e., supernatural), but is immanent within it, even though few can actually see it or experience it (i.e., paranatural).

So radical is the Upside Down's indifference to mundane human affairs that to call it antagonistic would be wrong. That word would imply some measure of concern, albeit hostile. The Upside Down isn't hostile per se (even if the Demogorgon is). Rather, it simply couldn't care any less. This notion is captured best by the opening sequence of episode 3, in which the Demogorgon violently drags Barb back into the Upside Down swimming pool. As she cries for her friend Nancy with bloodcurdling screams of terror, Foreigner's "I've Been Waiting for a Girl Like You" plays on the radio in Steve's bedroom, where Steve and Nancy are passionately kissing. The song eventually shifts from diegetic source music to non-diegetic underscoring, moving from a location within the narrative to some undisclosed location beyond or outside it. As it does, it continues on, unabated, entirely unconcerned with the unfolding violence. Here is the perfect audiovisual representation of the Upside Down: a radically indifferent cosmos, moving along mechanistically without any regard for the plight of humanity.

Once again, to think of the Upside Down as supernatural would be to misunderstand it, for in the world of *Stranger Things*, there simply is no such thing as super-nature. There are numerous overlapping dimensions of various sorts, which are all very mysterious, often terrifying, and in a very real sense haunted. But they are always concrete and material. If there is any hope for navigating such a world and, in some sense, overcoming its many horrors, the origin of this hope can't reside in any transcendent, otherworldly sphere of existence. No. In *Stranger Things*, hope, just like horror, can only ever emerge in and through immanent means.

The Horror of Hope

With everything that eventually unfolds over the course of the first season (including the tragic death of Barb), one might reasonably ask if the Right Side Up world is equally indifferent to the various traumas that mark the human condition. After all, if *Stranger Things* reveals anything, it's that real horror comes from within. More often than not, the things that go bump in the night either are the monsters of our own creation (government entities) or reveal the monster residing in all of us (Dr. Brenner).

But what is perhaps even more distressing is that, in *Stranger Things*, the victims of these horrors are almost always children and adolescents. Even though these young people are resilient in ways that adults simply cannot comprehend, they can never really escape the effects of their catastrophic encounters. Eleven is the most obvious example, but all of the kids in *Stranger Things* manifest signs of their trauma. Will, for example, comes back from the Upside Down alive, but he's not the same. In the closing moments of the season's final episode ("The Upside Down"), we see him vomit a disgusting mucous slug of some kind into the sink and then experience a brief vision of his bathroom walls being transformed into the Upside Down. It's unclear whether this all takes place in his head or if it in fact has some kind of ontic purchase, but it hardly matters. To be sure, Will has survived his originating trauma, but that can only mean one thing: he now exists in a fully post-traumatic state.

Given how pervasive this post-traumatic reality is in *Stranger Things*, the end of the first season comes as a bit of a surprise. But it's not the result of an unexpected plot twist. It's far more understated than that. The surprise is that, even though the narrative world has been turned upside down (in kata-strophic ways), the story points not toward a despairing nihilism, but to a hard-won hope rooted in self-giving love. It's an underlying narrative impulse that first emerges when Will attempts to fight off the Demogorgon in order to save his friends rather than protect himself, but it extends to all the other principal characters as well. Mike willingly jumps off a cliff to protect Dustin. Jonathan and Nancy both risk their lives to save Barb and each other. Hopper and Joyce do the same for Will. But the most overt demonstration of this self-giving love comes at the season 1 climax, when Eleven lays down her life not only to defeat the Demogorgon, but also to save her newfound friends. In fact, along with Nancy Wheeler and Joyce Byers, the female characters in the show outshine even the most virtuous of their male counterparts in demonstrating a kind of strength and commitment to sacrificial love.

Of course, in the context of late capitalist society, this kind of selfless love may strike some as either hollow or naïve, or maybe even both.[14] As a response to the profound horrors that plague the world, many consider love to be ineffective at best and, at worst, downright silly. From this view, the only thing more ridiculous than love itself would be the attendant hope that someone else might respond in kind. That's just not how the world works. To suggest otherwise, a contemporary viewer might respond, is to confuse fiction with reality.

Nevertheless, *Stranger Things* dares to hold out self-giving love as a real option in the modern world, even at the risk of sounding crazy. Because it's a fictionalized TV narrative riffing on the horror genre, it can get away with a lot. Viewers are willing to entertain the illogical and irrational, even if just for a moment, willing to suspend disbelief in order to encounter something that defies explanation. And therein lies the twist. The logic of love *is* absurd. Indeed, to place the well-being of another above one's own makes no rational sense. On the one hand, it may very well be that this notion of love simply reflects the fanciful thinking of the weak-minded and/or deluded. On the other hand, as far as meaningful responses to post-traumatic existence go, it might be the only real option—the only concrete hope. And if this is truly the case, then love is far more world-shattering, and hope is far more harrowing, than anyone could have possibly imagined.

Remember, the entire first season of the show takes place sometime between Thanksgiving and Christmas, a period of time that also overlaps with Advent on the Christian liturgical calendar. It's a season of expectant waiting. And from beginning to end, this hopeful anticipation is what haunts the world of *Stranger Things*, even if it goes largely unnamed and unacknowledged. Significantly though, it's a hope structured not by the absolute and eternal, but by the finite and conditional. In other words, the hope in *Stranger Things* doesn't have a transcendent source. Rather, it emerges in and through the immanent frame. As Hopper demonstrates when he leaves out Eggo waffles for Eleven (who disintegrated almost as quickly as she appeared), it's a kind of hope that risks a future that is yet to come—and in fact might never come, because no future is certain.

In more ways than one, *Stranger Things* locates the viewer in a world that is not merely riddled with uncertainty, but is haunted by monstrosities of various sorts. It's a world that has come face-to-(un)face with the unhuman. As such, it's a world in which there are no guarantees—except, that is, for further catastrophe. And in this permanent state of trauma, everything is contingent. No one, it would seem, is sure of what's to come. Indeed, given this context, the strangest thing about *Stranger Things* is not that it simply posits hope in the midst of a seemingly hopeless scenario. Rather, what is strange is that, much like the foreboding music that telegraphs the arrival of a creature just out of the camera's view, everything in the narrative points in this direction, yet hope still comes as a surprise. In certain respects, it's the most shocking element of the show—a jump scare of a different order. And it is for precisely this reason that it is difficult to imagine anything more horrifying than hope.

As Alasdair MacIntyre has suggested, "I can only answer the question 'What am I to do?' if I can answer the prior question 'Of what story or stories do I find myself a part?'"[15] *Stranger Things* isn't just another horror story. It's our story—the story in which contemporary people have been thrown. What it pictures so effectively is the common starting point for contemporary, post-secular life—the location from which an aesthetic of a/theism not only emerges, but also flourishes. It's a narrative world that is godless but not without mystery, immanent but not without the presence of the unhuman other, haunted but not without hope. And if it is accurate to suggest that this a/theistic sensibility is what constitutes the contemporary cultural landscape, the only question that remains is this: Given our location, what then are we to do?

Notes

1. We are borrowing the notion of being "haunted" by a "lost future" from Mark Fisher, *Ghosts of My Life: Writings on Depression, Hauntology and Lost Futures* (Washington, DC: Zero, 2014).

2. Jacques Derrida, "Faith and Knowledge: The Two Sources of Religion at the Limits of 'Reason' Alone," in *Religion: Cultural Memory in the Present* (Redwood City, CA: Stanford University Press, 1998).

3. As Douglas Cowan notes in his book *Sacred Terror*, this kind of religiously inflected, "supernatural" horror "remains a significant material disclosure of deeply embedded cultural fears of the supernatural and an equally entrenched ambivalence about the place and power of religion in society as the principal means of negotiating those fears." Douglas Cowan, *Sacred Terror: Religion and Horror on the Silver Screen* (Waco, TX: Baylor University Press, 2008), 9.

4. Eugene Thacker notes that Lovecraft's horror fiction betrays "a sense of wonder, of the mysterious—even, dare we say, of a religious quality—but a religiousness in the absence of any God whatsoever." Eugene Thacker, *Tentacles Longer Than Night:*, Horror of Philosophy, 3 (Washington, DC: Zero, 2014), 3:119.

5. Note here that, even though space will not allow us to make it explicit at all times, we are primarily employing the analytical tools set forth in Kutter Callaway and Dean Batali, *Watching TV Religiously: Television and Theology in Dialogue* (Grand Rapids: Baker Academic, 2016). Our TV analyses have also been significantly informed by Jason Mittell, *Complex TV: The Poetics of Contemporary Television Storytelling* (New York: New York University Press, 2015).

6. Henry Jenkins suggests that the upending of the hierarchy between media producers and media consumers paved the way for the emergence of what Jenkins now refers to as "participatory culture"—a shift driven in part by technological proliferation. Henry Jenkins, *Convergence Culture: Where Old and New Media Collide* (New York: New York University Press, 2006).

7. Taylor very clearly defines what he means by "secular" and, perhaps even more importantly, what he does *not* mean. What he does not

mean by "secular" is the diminished role of traditional religious institutions in the public sphere, which he calls "secularity 1." He also does not mean the (very real) phenomenon of decreasing religious belief and religious practice, a phenomenon he categorizes as "secularity 2." Instead, he employs the term *secular* (specifically "secular 3") to describe the present cultural conditions in which belief in God is no longer dominant, but contested, and unbelief is a viable option. In this way, secularity has to do more with the background conditions of belief than the content of those beliefs (or lack thereof). See Charles Taylor, *A Secular Age* (Cambridge, MA: Harvard University Press, 2007), 15.

8. "Non-diegetic" music is music that underscores the diegetic world (i.e., the enclosed narrative world of the characters) but does not have its source within that world. It serves as a buffer between the narrative and the audience, existing in a symbolic realm most often occupied by the implied narrator. As such, this kind of music is principally "for" the audience, offering viewers a particular take on the unfolding events within the narrative world.

9. We might also note the times in which the characters cry out in terror, "Oh, my God!," exclaim in anger "God help me," or sigh with relief, "Thank God." These represent another indeterminate yet strong vestige of theistic transcendence. We owe this insight to Joshua Beckett.

10. In this way, *Stranger Things* demonstrates how an otherwise speculative philosophical discourse finds its way into the contemporary cultural imagination. Although the likes of Heidegger, Gadamer, and Ricoeur initiated the turn to hermeneutics, the shift from "belief" to "hermeneutics" can also be found in the work of American thinkers, e.g., Van A. Harvey, *Feuerbach and the Interpretation of Religion: Cambridge Studies in Religion and Critical Thought* (New York: Cambridge University Press, 1995).

11. Chion describes the *acousmêtre* as an "acousmatic character whose relationship to the screen involves a specific kind of ambiguity and oscillation. . . . We may define it as neither inside nor outside the image. It is not inside, because the image of the voice's source—the body, the mouth—is not included. Nor is it outside, since it is not clearly positioned offscreen in an imaginary 'wing,' like a master of ceremonies or a witness, and it is implicated in the action, constantly about to be part of it. . . . [The *acousmêtre*] is an entire category of

characters . . . whose wholly specific presence is based on their very absence from the core of the image." Michel Chion, *Audio-Vision: Sound on Screen* (New York: Columbia University Press, 1994), 129.

12. Chion continues, "Why is the sight of the face necessary to de-acousmatization? For one thing, because the face represents the individual in her singularity. For another, the sight of the speaking face attests through the synchrony of audition/vision that the voice really belongs to that character, and thus is able to capture, domesticate, and 'embody' her (and humanize her as well)." Chion, *Audio-Vision*, 130.

13. The notion of the "unhuman" is taken from Eugene Thacker. We will return to this concept and engage in a more substantive interaction with Thacker's work in the next chapter. See Eugene Thacker, *In the Dust of This Planet*, Horror of Philosophy 1 (Washington, DC: Zero, 2011).

14. According to Alain Badiou, love is actually under threat in various domains of contemporary life, in large part because of the emergence of a "safety-first" concept of love—one that is "comprehensively insured against all risks." For Badiou, love "cannot be a gift given on the basis of a complete lack of risk," which is why love needs reinventing. Alain Badiou, *In Praise of Love* (New York: New Press, 2012), 6–7. Significantly, it is precisely this kind of risky, self-giving love that *Stranger Things* posits as the only viable response to the horrors of the modern world.

15. Alasdair MacIntyre, *After Virtue*, 3rd ed. (Notre Dame, IN: Notre Dame University Press, 2007), 216.

2

A Poetics of the Numinous

News headlines are not for the faint of heart. The looming threat of nuclear war, the easy alliance between heads of state and their totalitarian counterparts, the rise of neofascism and white nationalism—if humans are not monsters, they are, at the very least, utterly monstrous. Whether it's in the form of a government, a hallowed institution, society at large, or even individual persons, the human capacity to unleash terror upon the world and its inhabitants is unmatched. There isn't even a close second. In light of these actual horrors, horror stories would seem to be either superfluous or simply beside the point. Nevertheless, they continue to captivate the contemporary cultural imagination, nourished as they are by the reality of terror and the terror of reality.

That being said, audiences encounter a story like *Stranger Things* as horrifying not merely because it implies that humans might be the real monsters. It's also because of the prospect of coming face-to-face (or face-to-no-face) with something altogether different—something decidedly *un*human. In this way, to experience horror is to brush up against what theologian Rudolf Otto called the numinous. According to Otto, the numinous is an inherently religious category, but not because it contains some kind of specific religious content. Rather, the numinous is religious because it describes an encounter with the *mysterium tremendum et fascinans*. It's an overwhelming, impenetrable mystery (*mysterium*), one that is equal parts terrifying (*tremendum*) and alluring (*fascinans*).[1]

If the narrative world of *Stranger Things* is any indication, numinous encounters such as these are as prevalent today as they have ever been. It's just that now they are located in the wholly material world of late-modern life, which is largely closed off to any notion of transcendence. As a consequence, rather than go upward or outward to understand these inexplicable phenomena, contemporary persons have no other choice but to go downward and inward. For many if not most contemporary people, the numinous is neither supernatural nor superhuman. Nor is it necessarily (or even usually) benevolent or moral. Instead, it is a catastrophic excess that continues to overturn human life, churning just beneath the surface, leaving no one unscathed.

Thus, to meaningfully engage the various traumas of contemporary life, explorations of faith and doubt in the current context must challenge and ultimately move beyond the false dichotomy of belief/unbelief (along with transcendence/immanence and presence/absence). Moving in this direction is not about developing tidy analytic categories for classifying the horrific or the catastrophic, but constructing something along the lines of a poetics of the numinous—that is, an embodied, affective, sensual engagement with reality. More intuitive than deductive, this approach toward the numinous acknowledges that art and aesthetics make present certain aspects of existence that are otherwise absent or inaccessible. And it is this very poetic sensibility—one that persists even in the midst of a supposedly disenchanted world—that constitutes the aesthetics of a/theism.

What is more, if concrete cultural artifacts like *Stranger Things* do in fact embody the trauma that haunts the contemporary imagination, then, as a unique manifestation of material culture, horror fiction demonstrates how a/theism finds its way into the world of the mundane and everyday.[2] Indeed, it is largely for this reason that the horror genre serves as such a critical resource for capturing the zeitgeist of folk a/theism. For on a purely conceptual level, certain a/theistic notions are nonsensical—self-negating paradoxes. For instance, it simply makes no logical sense for the unhuman creature in *Stranger Things* to be neither supernatural nor natural (it has to be one or the other!). But in terms of the show's aesthetics, it makes all the sense in the world.

Interestingly enough, the same can be said for theology—especially the negative theology of the mystics. In fact, as philosopher of horror Eugene Thacker points out, the Christian mystical tradition offers what may be the closest analogy to the a/theistic self-negation embodied by the horror genre, primarily because the mystics explore not just the limitations of language, but the horizons of human thought as it confronts the "unthought."[3] Negative theology (sometimes called apophatic theology) operates with the assumption that human words are utterly incapable of describing God, so God must be approached indirectly and in terms of negation. To speak of or about God (i.e., *theologos*, literally a "god-word"), one can only say what God is not, never what God is. In other words, before it is anything else, negative theology (and perhaps all of theology rightly understood) is also a poetics of the numinous—a creative engagement with the terrifying mystery that hides in a kind of superfluous excess within the phenomenal world.[4] It isn't about acquiring more knowledge or information about God, but entering a great cloud of unknowing in and through increasingly imaginative modes of inquiry.

Needless to say, it would be one thing to claim that, given these similarities, atheism is simply parasitic upon the Christian tradition (which in some cases it is). It would be yet another to suggest that atheism provides theology with much-needed insight regarding the structures of belief that condition the contemporary cultural consciousness (which in most cases it does). But it is something altogether different to suggest that atheism and theology need each other. They are parallel projects that frequently overlap and, at times, even merge. They are partners and allies. Indeed, on the concrete level of lived experience, the boundaries between "theism" and "atheism" have become increasingly blurred, if not entirely dissolved, which has less to do with what people do or do not believe, and far more to do with a set of emerging cultural conditions in which the categories of belief/unbelief and theism/atheism are simply no longer intelligible.

Thus, to put it bluntly, if theology has any hope of addressing the profound crises that constitute modern life, it must learn to articulate Christianity in ways that contemporary people can understand and, ultimately, find meaningful. It is for this very reason that an exploration of the aesthetic dimensions of horror fiction is not simply an instructive exercise, but an imperative one. On a purely formal level, the horror genre demonstrates how an ostensibly a/theistic cultural product can offer people of diverse religious (and non-religious) commitments a shared resource for making sense of their catastrophic encounters with the *mysterium tremendum et fascinans*. *Stranger Things* is but one of the more prominent examples of the genre functioning in precisely this way, for it provides the necessary language, images, and symbols for redescribing reality in light of an encounter with the Upside Down.

However, to understand more fully how a pop-cultural artifact like *Stranger Things* actually establishes these new symbolic coordinates and, thereby, enables contemporary people to navigate post-secular life, it is vital to listen to and learn from the right set of interlocutors. Philosophers of atheism like Eugene Thacker and Mark C. Taylor provide the most helpful tools for describing and assessing the aesthetics of a/theism, while also granting insight into the question of why anyone (whether theist, atheist, or none of the above) would want to do so in the first place. Their conceptual categories not only generate richer interpretations of the artifact in question, but also name what is often overlooked or, perhaps more accurately, cannot even be seen from a purely theological perspective.

Horror as Paralogical

In his Horror of Philosophy series, Eugene Thacker poses what seems to be a rhetorical question: What if this thing called "the world" doesn't revolve around human beings? What if, in actual fact, it wants nothing to do with humans at all? That, says Thacker, is a truly terrifying thought. From this view, the horror genre is not merely about the evocation of fear, whether visceral, psychosomatic, or existential. Rather, horror is horrifying because it deals with the limits of the human as it confronts the "world-without-us."[5] To posit this kind of a world—one that is not simply unknown but is wholly unknowable—is to open up a radical uncertainty. Or to put it somewhat differently, whatever fear horror does induce is rooted in its attempt to think the "unhuman."

At first blush, this idea of a world-without-us that is as unknowable as it is unhuman appears to be neither logical nor rational. And that's because it isn't logical or rational. But neither is it *ir*rational or *il*logical. Instead, it's paralogical and para-rational. It runs alongside of and parallel to reason, rather than in contradiction to it. That is to say, rather than being either/or or both/and, it's neither/nor. But to understand how the paralogic of the unhuman operates in the context of horror fiction, one needs a decidedly aesthetic competence and sensibility. Here, poetic intuitions are more valuable than logical syllogisms, in large part because aesthetic experiences are uniquely able to hold seemingly opposing realities in creative tension without one giving way to the other. In ways that other forms of knowledge production simply cannot replicate, art (including horror fiction) generates an aesthetic unity constituted by relational rather than oppositional difference. In so doing, art has the capacity to make present that which is absent: paradoxical revelations of divine darkness in a cultural context where not only is god dead but the world itself is no longer for the humans who inhabit it.

The Unhuman as the World-without-Us

The first and perhaps most immediately useful category Thacker identifies is known as the "world-without-us" or, more simply, the "unhuman." This conceptual tool is uniquely helpful for describing, analyzing, and understanding one of the primary aesthetic features of the horror genre and, indeed, one of its core paradoxes. Thacker suggests that, in horror fiction, the world "as it is in itself" is only ever revealed as that which is hidden, unknowable, and by definition outside the scope of human comprehension. As a consequence, the only knowledge this revelation produces is that of humanity's limitations. It is knowledge of the world as "essentially hidden, rather than given (religion) or produced (science)."[6] In this way, the genre of horror is doing something akin to philosophy, but "in so far as it evokes the world-without-us as a limit, it is a 'negative philosophy' (akin to negative theology, but in the absence of God)."[7]

Conceptually, then, Thacker approaches the horror genre as humanity's attempt to grapple with a radically indifferent cosmos not through abstractions and logical rigor, but in and through material culture. The implicit philosophy of these concrete aesthetic productions (e.g., film, TV, literary fiction) is negative in the sense that it challenges the often unacknowledged assumption that makes any philosophical and, by extension, theological inquiry possible. Namely, horror dares to question the most basic presumption of the modern project—the notion that the world is always the world-for-us. As a kind of negative theology sans God, horror calls out the sheer hubris of assuming that humans inhabit a thoroughly human-centric world.[8]

Indeed, the contrast between horror and most other modern discourses is both stark and unsettling. For instance, according to Thacker, the commonality between modern religion and modern empirical science is not simply that they seek after the world because they both assume it to be meaningful (either because meaning is given in the created order or because it can be produced through scientific discovery), but that they operate with a fully anthropocentric view of the world. Horror moves in the polar opposite direction. It entertains the possibility that there may very well be no reason for something existing in the first place, and that the world is not only "indifferent to us, but that the world is and has always been mostly an inhuman world."[9] This is by no means "a comforting thought," says Thacker, "but then again, neither philosophy, nor religion, nor horror, is meant to comfort."[10]

Cosmic Pessimism and Disgust

A second category of horror has to do with the relationship between what Thacker calls "cosmic pessimism" and "disgust." Thacker prefers the term *cosmic pessimism* over nihilism because he sees horror as offering an alternative (and perhaps even an antidote) to the actual nihilism of modern religion and modern science, both of which attempt to give meaning to the world without acknowledging that, in light of the death of god, meaning making is a dead end.[11] This is why he resonates with horror authors like H. P. Lovecraft and, at the same time, can draw upon the conceptual schemes of the mystical theological tradition. In both cases, claims Thacker, there is an attempt to articulate a "basic relationship between the human being and the limits of its capacity to adequately comprehend the world in which it finds itself."[12] This first-order experience of human limitation and inadequacy is, in fact, why the visions of the Christian mystics are called "mystical" (taken from the Greek word *mysterion*, meaning "hidden"), for they are describing encounters with an unknown other that doesn't disclose so much as it shrouds itself in divine darkness, clouds of unknowing, and dark nights of the soul. In other words, both horror and mystical theology admit that reality is mostly nonconsensual; the world simply does not play along with anyone's attempt to know and thereby master it.

According to the conventions of the horror genre, the location where this hidden and nonconsensual world interfaces with the world as it is known is often some kind of magic site, which is "the place where the hiddenness of the world presents itself in its paradoxical way (revealing itself—as hidden)."[13] The interaction between these two worlds (i.e., the world-without-us and the world-for-us) generates unsettling effects, two of the more common being the appearance of mists and ooze. Whether it's ooze that attaches itself to a monster and provides the trail evidence of its former presence or it's a mist that hovers amorphously over a mysterious location, these strange manifestations signal the profound disgust—the allergic reaction—triggered by the meeting of these two worlds.

The reflexive sense of disgust generated by the presence of the unhuman (or the trail of ooze that marks its absence) indicates that fear alone is not the whole of what makes horror horrifying, especially as it concerns the viewer's emotional engagement with the genre. Indeed, from the perspective of the cognitive sciences, every interaction with the unhuman in horror fiction involves a basic level of revulsion. "Think of the zombies in *Night of the Living Dead* (1968), or the giant, dribbling snails in *The Monster That Challenged the World* (1957)," says Noël Carroll. "We find the monsters in horror films repulsive and abhorrent. They are not only fearsome, they are somehow unclean, reviling, and loathsome by their very nature."[14] More than a mere gag reflex, disgust is symptomatic of a much deeper and far more elemental fear of the unknown and unknowable other intruding into the world as it is known.

The Numinous

Third and finally, by developing the concept of the "numinous," Thacker addresses the way in which the revolting nature of this encounter with the unhuman presents a significant dilemma for everyone involved. Namely, the actual human beings who both watch and populate these horror stories are left with no other choice but to confront the world-without-us, but they must do so without presuming that it is identical to the world in which they exist and, at the same time, without falling into despair in the face of its sheer inaccessibility. Taken from this perspective, the core conflict that orients the horror genre as a whole (i.e., the confrontation between the human world-for-us and the unhuman world-without-us) bears many of the same markings as the numinous encounters that Rudolf Otto described in terms of the *mysterium tremendum et fascinans*. In Otto's accounting, these experiences involve a combination of horror, dread, fear (*tremendum*) and wonder, awe, allure (*fascinans*) because, at their most basic, they entail a confrontation with the absolutely nonhuman. To encounter the numinous is to come upon something "wholly other," something fundamentally not-for-the-human.[15]

Otto's formulation of the numinous not only provides a

useful description of the unhuman as it appears in contemporary horror fiction but also lays out a conceptual pathway for connecting Thacker's take on horror to the negative theology of Christian mysticism. According to Otto, the numinous is necessarily a negation—a void. In fact, any positive conceptual content attributed to it, such as "supernatural" or "transcendent," is largely superficial, for even these terms are negative attributes with reference to nature and the world or cosmos respectively.[16] In this way, the mysterious "beyond" of Christian mysticism functions not as a category of being that can be compared with the natural world as it exists "for" the human. Rather, the negative theology of the mystics dares to suggest that the divine itself is shrouded in apophatic darkness, encountered by humans only as "that which is nothing." Meister Eckhart, for instance, frequently invokes the terms "Godhead" or "the One" to speak of this enigmatic God-beyond-Being, which is his way of pushing toward a "non-anthropomorphic, non-anthropocentric notion of nothing/nothingness that is, at the same time, not separate from the human being."[17] To use Thacker's terminology, Eckhart's God-beyond-Being is, in the truest sense of the term, a God-without-us.

The Paralogic of a Mysticism without God

As conceptual tools, the world-without-us, the numinous, and the disgust they engender certainly dissolve the distinction between theism and atheism (along with rationality and irrationality). But it is the decidedly aesthetic shape of these symbolic resources that allow them to hold on to both the human and the unhuman without one running roughshod over the other. And as they do, new possibilities emerge not only for understanding the truly terrifying elements of a horror story like *Stranger Things*, but also for establishing a new set of coordinates for navigating the contemporary landscape—coordinates grounded in the thoroughgoing paralogic of an a/theistic aesthetic.

Nevertheless, to point out the apparent similarities between these categories and the religious traditions upon which they depend is not to suggest that contemporary horror is really just theism in disguise or that contemporary audiences are somehow unwitting theists. Thacker is not simply parroting the theology of Otto and Eckhart and calling it "philosophy." The interpretative categories he provides are resolutely non-theistic. In fact, his is an attempt to ask whether the genre might be functioning as a concrete manifestation of a "mysticism without God," which is a clear departure from the theologians upon whom he so often depends. In contrast to Thacker, Otto and Eckhart still preserve a basic distinction between two types of "nothing." In the terms established by their theology of negation, God is "no-thing" and, thus, cannot be known as such. But according to Thacker's notion of the divine, there just "is" nothing, so there is nothing to be known.[18]

It is not for nothing (pun intended) that this ever-so-slight distinction serves as the primary difference between Thacker and the apophatic theology he engages. He is not interested in advancing a philosophy of horror that is simply a secular version of theology or a reaffirmation of religious faith, in large part because his context is radically different than that of his theological forebears. But Thacker's is precisely the same context in which contemporary persons find themselves. As a consequence, contemporary horror does indeed emphasize the radical indifference of the unhuman world, but it too lands in a cultural context that is also "a godless world, a world that has been able to encompass both Nietzsche's 'death of God' and the return of religious fanaticisms of all types." In other words, horror embodies what might be called "a heretical type of mysticism, a mysticism without religion, a mysticism without God."[19]

All that remains in this secular, scientific, skeptical world is the world-shattering, catastrophic encounter with the numinous—an unknowable something that is neither transcendent nor immanent, neither supernatural nor natural.[20] The numinous can neither be "above" the natural nor be "underneath" it, because it is fundamentally unhuman, indifferent, and incomprehensible.

Lest the more theologically minded despair at this notion of a mysticism without God, it may be helpful to point out that, because it suspends the viewer in the space between the "normative, human world of scientific laws and therapeutic religion" and the "purely supernatural domain of the heavens or the underworld," horror calls for a daring kind of humility.[21] It presses viewers to muster the courage to admit one of two things regarding their encounters with the numinous: either it took place all in their heads, or it really happened. The numinous either doesn't exist (and so can be explained) or does exist (and cannot be explained).[22] Either way, humility is paramount if one is to embrace the fundamentally paralogical idea of a mysticism without god. If for no other reason, this impulse toward humility is reason enough to understand something of the aesthetics of the horror genre.

Neither Religion nor God

Thacker is not alone in his desire to construct a mysticism without God—one that rejects the absolute dualisms of transcendence/immanence and theism/atheism in favor of something more complex, relational, and emergent. In fact, this is Mark C. Taylor's explicitly stated goal in his book *After God*. Along strikingly similar lines to Thacker, Taylor suggests that, given the impact of religion on every aspect of culture, contemporary societies need to develop alternative religious schemata that avoid the historical tendency (at least in the West) either to make God "so transcendent that he is irrelevant or so immanent that there is no difference between the sacred and the secular."[23] Every religious vision, says Taylor, provides a way to imagine the real, which has direct implications for how human beings relate to nature, society, and culture.

Taylor is suggesting that, because contemporary people inhabit a world "after God," the only hope for addressing the crises, catastrophes, and traumas that constitute that world is to discover anew how to articulate and express that which cannot be represented: life itself. Doing so, however, requires something less like a scientific and religious dogma and something far more like an aesthetics of a/theism. Taylor's work helpfully clarifies why this is, in fact, the case and, by extension, why a show like *Stranger Things* might very well serve as an important resource for such an endeavor.

A Trinitarian Twist on the Human

In contrast to a both/and or an either/or way of imagining reality, Taylor proposes a third way: neither/nor.[24] At its most basic, Taylor's alternative schema conceives of the difference between immanence and transcendence not as oppositional, but as thoroughly relational. Even more importantly, this relationality bears a triadic structure. It is, to use explicitly theological language, trinitarian. Indeed, in Taylor's mind, the conceptual apparatus of the Trinity offers an alternative to pure immanence on the one hand and absolute transcendence on the other.

It is important to note, however, that even though Taylor's framework is trinitarian in terms of its structure, his starting point is not the Trinity per se. Rather, because it informs how one imagines and relates to the real, the most immediate implication of Taylor's neither/nor schema concerns the nature of the self.

According to Taylor, one of the primary difficulties with wholly materialist (i.e., both/and) and exclusively supernatural (i.e., either/or) conceptions of the world is that they can neither account for nor explain human self-consciousness in any nonreductive way.[25] It is one thing to be conscious. It is quite another to be aware of one's awareness—to be self-reflective and self-representational—and also to be aware of the self-consciousness of others. These are operations of the "mind" (itself a metaphor or symbol) that are not reducible to material explanations. No straight causal line can be drawn from neurophysiological processes (the material cause) to these various forms of human consciousness (the immaterial effect). And to move in the other direction, from effect to cause (as hardcore materialists do), is to traffic in purely hypothetical inference while smuggling the immaterial in through the back door. In other words, a linear, both/and approach is incapable of recognizing that the physiological manifestation of self-awareness is a symptom of that which is immaterial and perhaps even hidden.[26]

In contrast to flattened, linear models of this sort, Taylor's triadic schema understands human personhood as emerging only when the self-as-subject and self-as-object join together in a kind of unity of negative self-relation. That is, neither the subjective "I" nor the objective "me" can be fully itself apart from the other. But neither are they identical. They are rather fundamentally related in and through difference, so neither one can precede or posit the other. In this way, self-relation, says Taylor, "presupposes a third."[27] "I" relate to "me" in and through "myself"—an unnamed Other that is neither present nor absent. Because this relation is located in the depths of human interiority, it is profoundly immanent. At the same time, because it posits an unknowable Other, it is irreducibly transcendent. Thus, much like the God of orthodox Trinitarian theology, the human, it would seem, is also fundamentally relational.

The World as a Work of Art

Taylor builds upon this self-relational conception of personhood by suggesting that the mysterious Other hidden within the depths of human self-consciousness also serves as the "infinite background that is the origin of the work of art."[28] When viewed through a triadic schema, the creative imagination and human subjectivity are structurally isomorphic, which may at least partly explain why the mysteries of human personhood so often call for poetic expression and exploration. Indeed, it is only through poetics broadly understood as the creating and making of forms (i.e., *poiesis*) that humans are able to articulate or come to know much of anything about the world at all.

For Taylor, then, the poetic imagination is critical because it serves as the primary (and perhaps only) resource for grappling with the unthinkable alternative between theism and atheism, transcendence and immanence, belief and unbelief. It recasts what seem to be oppositional differences in terms of a fundamentally relational identity. Just as human personhood emerges from a self-contradiction that is inwardly differentiated yet unified, a creative work of art demonstrates not a mathematical uniformity but an organic unity that allows for the simultaneous existence of complex differences.[29] In fact, given their complex and variegated nature, neither the depths of human subjectivity nor the profound effects of a beautiful work of art can be fully expressed in arithmetic or propositional terms. They can only be expressed in and through aesthetic means, which are fundamentally relational.

Consider Thacker's illuminating take on darkness as both a phenomenon and a poetic means for figuring forth what cannot be articulated or represented, namely, the presence of an absence. Darkness "is" something in its own right but at the same time "is not" light. It exists, but only as the absence of its opposite.[30] Darkness is therefore an absence that is, at the same time, "there." It is present in ways that anyone who has ever been afraid of the dark can confirm, even if it is quite literally a no-thing at all.

As such, although its operations are decidedly poetic, darkness as a no-thing engenders a kind of horror that is more than merely metaphorical. Indeed, one of the truly terrifying aspects of this absent presence is that it is always realized in material form. Philosopher Calvin L. Warren makes this point devastatingly clear in his *Ontological Terror: Blackness, Nihilism, and Emancipation*.[31] For Warren, black bodies quite literally incarnate (i.e., embody) the nothing or nonbeing that is necessary to sustain the metaphysical world of modernity. Black being exists to not exist, and the history of violence enacted upon this nothing-that-is-a-something is a direct and tangible manifestation of this negation. The perpetual trauma inflicted upon black bodies is perhaps the most horrific and horrifying example of how the aesthetics of a/theism translates into the poetics of the world. Blackness cannot ground itself in human being, for it exists as the absence or negation of the human. It thus is not—indeed, cannot be—human, and neither a liberal progressivism nor a humanistic optimism can address this horror. From Warren's perspective, the only solution to this situation is the end of the world. The only hope, if there is such a thing, is an imaginative, poetic reconstruction of reality.

In a distinct though strikingly similar way, self-negating forms of artistic representation are most capable of articulating what are otherwise philosophical or logical dead ends.[32] Take, for instance, the use of the color black in art. It's "a 'color' that is not really a color—a color that either negates or consumes all colors."[33] In other words, what can only exist as a contradiction in logical terms (i.e., darkness both "is" and "is not"; the self is both a "subject" and an "object"), works of art can hold together in the form of an organic unity—an aesthetic coherence that viewers encounter on both formal and phenomenological levels.

Where Art and Religion Meet

Taylor could stop here—by pointing out the structural similarities between aesthetic encounters and self-consciousness—but he doesn't, in large part because his theoretical framework demands that he follow this line of thought to its logical conclusion. Thus, for Taylor, these structures aren't merely triadic in some superficial (or arithmetic) sense. Rather, they are expressly *Trinitarian*, which means that the neither/nor schema is inexorably linked to the theological tradition that bears this same designation. And from this particular view, a basic relationality not only structures human subjectivity and the process of creating and engaging art, but it also strikes "at the very heart of the Christian notion of God."[34]

Taylor rightly credits Augustine as being the first to recognize the similarity between self-consciousness and the Trinitarian God. Augustine was a fourth-century African bishop whose theological vision was deeply shaped by Neoplatonism (a school of thought that imagined all of reality emanating from and ultimately reuniting with a deity known as "The One"). Like any good Neoplatonist, he begins with God as triune and develops all of his subsequent theological categories from this starting point. For Augustine, then, because God is triune, the basic relationality that constitutes the inner-Trinitarian life of the Godhead also constitutes the whole of the created order. In other words, the structure of all reality is triadic because God is.

Even though certain defenders of orthodoxy might quibble with Taylor's interpretation of Augustine, the end result is that he freely draws upon orthodox Trinitarian theology as a resource for constructing his poetics of the numinous. Indeed, for Taylor, the incarnation, which necessarily requires the doctrine of the Trinity (and vice versa), is the ultimate embodiment of the neither/nor principle of relationalism in which identity is understood to be differential rather than oppositional. Accordingly, "The triadic structure of Father-Son-Spirit is isomorphic with the triadic structure of self-consciousness: self-as-subject (Father), self-as-object (Son), and the interrelation of the two (Spirit)."[35]

When understood in these terms, the structure of human subjectivity corresponds not only to works of art, but also to the Trinitarian God, for each represents "the structure of self-referentiality or self-reflexivity in which apparent opposites are reciprocally related in a way that renders them coemergent and codependent."[36] In other words, the internal structures shared in common by God, humans, and art are fundamentally relational. They create the necessary conditions for a unity-in-difference to emerge. Art and religion, then, meet in life, which itself is both structurally and substantively Trinitarian. And if this is indeed the case, then to sustain life is to cultivate all of these complex relations. It is to create art (*poiesis*), which figures and disfigures the visions that shape human experience and pattern the world.[37]

Here, then, is where Taylor and Thacker's adaptive schemata serve as helpful tools not only for describing the narrative world of *Stranger Things*, but also for understanding the ways in which the show's formal aesthetic provides viewers with a resource for addressing the traumas of modern life. It is by no means incidental that the Christian theological tradition plays a helpful role in navigating an increasingly post-secular culture. But the a/theistic vision of a show like *Stranger Things* is still a far cry from dogmatic theology. It's much more like the portal to the Upside Down—a gateway that both opens up and makes present certain aspects of reality that are otherwise inaccessible, namely, the inexpressible, inexhaustible mystery that is existence itself.

Love without Conditions

It is important to point out that both Taylor and Thacker are developing interpretive frameworks for describing and critically engaging with the human condition. So even when they are proposing philosophical constructs like "immanent transcendence," they are theorizing about the phenomena known as "immanence" and "transcendence." What they are not doing (at least not intentionally) is developing any kind of orthodox confessional theology. They deploy "immanent transcendence" almost entirely as a phenomenological category and most decidedly not as a metaphysical one, which means that the analogy between their a/theological projects and what most people mean by Christian or religious "faith" is largely formal.[38]

Bearing all of this in mind, both Thacker and Taylor are, in their own ways, constructing parallel visions for negotiating the complex and contradictory terrain of twenty-first-century life.[39] The distinctions between what counts as theological or a/theological should not be drawn too sharply here, especially given this shared desire to reconstruct a more life-giving vision in the face of nihilism and despair. In other words, given the common space they inhabit, the theist and a/theist—those who believe and those who do not—need each other, perhaps now more than ever. For it is one thing to develop the category of "immanent transcendence" as an object of intellectual or philosophical inquiry. It is quite another to commit oneself to the numinous in love. Of course, to speak not simply of "knowing" but of loving this mysterious darkness is to shift into a decidedly aesthetic register. It is to wax poetic, to engage in *poiesis*. But then again, that's entirely the point. Both atheism and theism are, at their core, aesthetic visions, so it only makes sense that, in an ultimate sense, they are drawn together in and through the poetic allure of love.

To quote French philosopher Alain Badiou, "Love is the hidden power within the catastrophe [of existence]."[40] It is both pervasive and fundamentally obscure, because it is hidden within the very structures of our world. Through love, one experiences the world from the viewpoint of another, which is why it is an experience of decentering, distinction, and disjunction.[41] Badiou even goes so far as to say that "every love states that it is eternal. . . . Because, basically, that is what love is: a declaration of eternity to be fulfilled or unfurled as best it can be within time: eternity descending into time."[42]

Rooted as it is in catastrophe, love reaches out toward the other and even takes up the viewpoint of the other. It is a declaration of eternity descending into time. Here, Badiou's work, much like Thacker's and Taylor's, is explicitly theological and, at times, even incarnational. It, too, is a kind of poetics of the numinous—an aesthetic engagement with the mysterious something that seems to pervade and animate the whole of life. But also like Thacker and Taylor, Badiou is quick to point out that his notion of love is not dependent upon any kind of absolute transcendence per se. To be sure, it is a universal affirmation of concrete encounters with difference and "otherness," but this is not an "Almighty-Other" or "Great-Other."[43] Like Thacker's "mysticism without religion" and Taylor's "religion without God," Badiou's is a "love without conditions."

This then is where the a/theological rubber meets the road, so to speak. Badiou's notion of love augments Thacker's and Taylor's neither/nor logic by carving out a space within the contemporary landscape in which the religious imagination might flourish. Of course, in a world that has experienced the death of god, love's eternal referents might remain forever "quasi-eternal." But as Badiou suggests, because love is the hidden power within the catastrophic—the absent center of the traumatic real—it can be neither absolutely transcendent nor purely immanent, but is rather the reinvention of life itself.[44]

Needless to say, to keep this neither/nor space from collapsing into pure immanence, people of genuine religious faith need to stay committed to the conversation. It is certainly true that a/theological projects can and do serve as invaluable resources for theological dialogue, in large part because they keep people of religious faith honest. It is all too easy for otherwise-thoughtful Christians to lose themselves in the transcendent realm of an either/or dualism and thus to forget the relational dynamics of both the triune God and their concrete lives. In the same way, confessional theology can prove to be a helpful resource to the a/theologian insofar as it serves as a constant reminder not to reduce transcendence to such a degree that it no longer means much of anything to anyone.

In sum: Contemporary horror fiction locates viewers in a context defined not by the supernatural but by the unhuman world-without-us, which means that theology desperately needs to identify new coordinates for navigating this new reality. Insofar as it embodies a distinctly a/theistic aesthetic, a show like *Stranger Things* serves as one potential resource for an endeavor of this kind. Not only does it allow viewers to hold together multiple competing realities without one giving way to the others, but it also demonstrates that the only viable response to the catastrophes and horrors of the world is a kind of self-othering love. To be sure, *Stranger Things*, like most contemporary horror, knows nothing of the absolutely transcendent God of classic Christian orthodoxy. It depicts a "mysticism without religion," a "religion without God," and a "love without conditions." But make no mistake; it is still mysticism. It is still religion. It is, above all, still love. And in this way, horror fiction presents its own poetics of the numinous capable of confronting the traumatic real—a means by which to move forward in a world without god.

Notes

1. Rudolf Otto, *The Idea of the Holy*, 2nd ed., trans. John W. Harvey (New York: Oxford University Press, 1950).

2. Following this line of thought, this chapter borrows heavily from the work of Eugene Thacker, who has recently written a trilogy of books on the connection between philosophy and the genre of horror "as it is manifest in fiction, film, comics, music, and other media." Eugene Thacker, *In the Dust of This Planet*, Horror of Philosophy 1 (Winchester, UK: Zero, 2011), 1.

3. Thacker, *In the Dust of This Planet*, 47.

4. Peter Rollins calls this superfluous excess "hypernymity." Peter Rollins, *How (Not) to Speak of God* (Brewster, MA: Paraclete, 2006).

5. Thacker, *In the Dust of This Planet*, 8.

6. Thacker, *In the Dust of This Planet*, 66.

7. Thacker, *In the Dust of This Planet*, 9.

8. Eugene Thacker, *Tentacles Longer Than Night,* Horror of Philosophy 3 (Winchester, UK: Zero, 2015), 11.

9. Thacker, *Tentacles Longer Than Night*, 20.

10. Thacker, *Tentacles Longer Than Night*, 20.

11. "Our response . . . should not be to rediscover some new ground for giving meaning to the world, be it in religious or scientific terms, and neither should we be satisfied to wallow in despair at this loss of meaning, this 'abyss of nihility.' Instead, we should delve deeper into this abyss, this nothingness, which may hold within a way out of the dead end of nihilism." Thacker, *In the Dust of This Planet*, 156–57.

12. Thacker, *Tentacles Longer Than Night*, 19.

13. Thacker, *In the Dust of This Planet*, 82.

14. Noël Carroll, "Film, Emotion, and Genre," in *Passionate Views: Film, Cognition, and Emotion*, ed. Carl Plantinga and Greg M. Smith (Baltimore: Johns Hopkins University Press, 1999), 39–40.

15. "The truly 'mysterious' object is beyond our apprehension and comprehension, not only because our knowledge has certain irremovable limits, but because in it we come upon something inherently 'wholly other,' whose kind and character are incommensurable with our own, and before which we therefore

85

recoil in a wonder that strikes us chill and numb." Otto, *The Idea of the Holy*, 28.

16. Otto, *The Idea of the Holy*, 30.

17. Eugene Thacker, *Starry Speculative Corpse*, Horror of Philosophy 2 (Winchester, UK: Zero, 2015), 17.

18. Thacker, *Starry Speculative Corpse*, 42.

19. Thacker, *Tentacles Longer Than Night*, 127.

20. Following Thacker, we prefer the term "numinous" instead of "supernatural" because the logic of the numinous is structured not by any kind of relation to the natural world (i.e., super-natural), but rather by the impossibility of this relation.

21. Thacker, *In the Dust of This Planet*, 81.

22. "Either the phenomena [*sic*] in question can be explained according to the accepted laws of nature (and it doesn't really exist), or else it cannot be explained (and does exist)." Thacker, *Tentacles Longer Than Night*, 165.

23. Mark C. Taylor, *After God* (Chicago: University of Chicago Press, 2007), xvi.

24. "The complex type is the third religious schema. In contrast to the monistic and dualistic types, the real in this case is neither present nor absent; rather, it is irreducibly interstitial or liminal and as such is *virtual*. . . . The virtual is not simply the possible but is the *matrix* in which possibility and actuality emerge. . . . Always betwixt and between, it is neither immanent nor transcendent—neither here and now nor elsewhere and beyond. To the contrary, the virtual is something like an immanent transcendence." Taylor, *After God*, 40–41.

25. "The reluctance to engage in critical reflection on the nature of religion has led to an interpretive vacuum that has been filled by a variety of reductive analyses in which religion is understood as a mere epiphenomenon of more basic or fundamental processes." Taylor, *After God*, 5.

It should be noted that Taylor is certainly not alone in this regard. For instance, according to Thacker, "Eliminative materialism questions the existence of 'qualia' such as mental states, psychological behaviors, or subjective affects. At its most extreme, it challenges any claims for an independently-existing mind beyond neurological and biological basis. . . . At its extreme, the search for a material basis for life (be it in a molecule or even, ironically, in biological 'information') ends up reducing life to its material constituents—at which point there is no life at all." Thacker, *Starry Speculative Corpse*, 46–148.

Similarly, as neuroscientist and philosopher Raymond Tallis suggests, "Naturalist, which are ultimately materialistic, explanations are currently in the ascendant in secular circles. But they leave consciousness, self-consciousness, the self, free will, the community of minds and most features of the human world unexplained. Supernatural explanations just parcel up our uncertainties in the notion of an entity—God—that is not only unexplained, but usually contradictory." Raymond Tallis, *In Defence of Wonder, and Other Philosophical Reflections* (Durham, UK: Acumen, 2012), as cited in Graham Ward, *Unbelievable: Why We Believe and Why We Don't* (New York: Tauris, 2014), 194.

The problems with pure materialism are, of course, not new, but they are particularly pressing in our increasingly "scientistic" cultural setting. William James, the father of American psychology, noted some of these difficulties at the end of the nineteenth century: "Medical materialism seems indeed a good appellation for the too simple-minded system of thought which we are considering. . . . Let us ourselves look at the matter in the largest possible way. Modern psychology, finding definite psycho-physical connections to hold good, assumes as a convenient hypothesis that the dependence of mental states upon bodily conditions must be thoroughgoing and complete. If we adopt the assumption, then of course what medical materialism insists on must be true in a general way, if not in every detail: Saint Paul certainly had once an epileptoid, if not an epileptic seizure. . . . But now, I ask you, how can such an existential account of facts of mental history decide in one way or another upon their spiritual significance? According to the general postulate of psychology just referred to, there is not a single one of our states of mind, high or low, healthy or morbid, that has not some organic process as its condition. Scientific theories are organically conditioned just as much as religious emotions are; and if we only knew the facts intimately enough, we should doubtless see 'the liver' determining the dicta of the sturdy atheist as decisively as it does those of the Methodist under conviction anxious about his soul." William James, *The Varieties of Religious Experience: A Study in Human Nature*, Kindle ed. (Heraklion Press, 2014), 11–12.

26. As Graham Ward says, these physiological manifestations are

"symptoms and signs of that which remains, fundamentally, hidden." Ward, *Unbelievable*, 193.

27. "In the depths of [human] interiority lies hidden an Other than can never be known. Though nothing is closer to consciousness, this Other is not personal but remains an unnamable anonymity that shadows subjectivity. . . . Since the relation and the *relata* are codependent, neither can posit the other. Self-relation, therefore, presupposes a third. . . . In relating itself to itself, the self inevitably but unknowingly relates itself to an Other, which is neither present nor absent." Taylor, *After God*, 120.

28. Here he is developing the work of both Heidegger and Coleridge. Taylor, *After God*, 121.

29. Taylor, *After God*, 152.

30. "Darkness is at once something negative, and yet, presenting itself as such, is also something positive; from a philosophical perspective, darkness exists, but its existence is always tenuous, the stuff of shadows, night, and tenebrous clouds. Darkness 'is' but also 'is not'—and, in a way, this 'is not' also 'is' darkness. Put simply, the concept of darkness invites us to think about this basic philosophical dilemma of a nothing that is a something." Thacker, *Starry Speculative Corpse*, 17–18.

31. Calvin L. Warren, *Ontological Terror: Blackness, Nihilism, and Emancipation* (Durham, NC: Duke University Press, 2018).

32. The primary distinction, according to Warren, is that blackness is an index of formlessness, whereas the color black assumes a sensible form within metaphysics. Warren, *Ontological Terror*, 34.

33. Thacker, *Starry Speculative Corpse*, 49 (emphasis in original).

34. Taylor, *After God*, 158.

35. Taylor, *After God*, 160–61.

36. Taylor, *After God*, 158.

37. Taylor, *After God*, 343.

38. Underscoring a similar set of subtle differences between philosophers of a/theism and negative theology, Caputo states, "Negative theology is always on the track of a 'hyperessentiality,' of something hyper-present, hyper-real or sur-real, so really real that we are never satisfied simply to say that it is merely real. *Différance*, on the other hand, is less real than real, not quite real, never gets as

far as being or entity or presence, which is why it is emblematized by insubstantial quasi-beings like ashes and ghosts which flutter between existence and nonexistence, or with humble *khôra*, say, rather than with the prestigious Platonic sun. *Différance* is but a quasi-transcendental anteriority, not a supereminent, transcendent ulteriority." John D. Caputo, *The Prayers and Tears of Jacques Derrida: Religion without Religion* (Indianapolis: Indiana University Press, 1997), 2–3.

39. Taylor, *After God*, 42.

40. Alain Badiou with Nicolas Truong, *In Praise of Love*, trans. Peter Bush (New York: New Press, 2012), 83.

41. Love "reaches out towards the ontological," for it focuses not on "particular objects, but . . . on the being of the other, on the other as it has erupted, fully armed with its being, into my life thus disrupted and re-fashioned." Badiou, *In Praise of Love*, 21.

42. Badiou, *In Praise of Love*, 47.

43. Badiou, *In Praise of Love*, 66.

44. Badiou, *In Praise of Love*, 33.

3

The Empty Tomb as God's Absence

When the Sabbath was over, Mary Magdalene, Mary the mother of James, and Salome bought aromatic spices so that they might go and anoint him. And very early on the first day of the week, at sunrise, they went to the tomb. They had been asking each other, "Who will roll away the stone for us from the entrance to the tomb?" But when they looked up, they saw that the stone, which was very large, had been rolled back. Then as they went into the tomb, they saw a young man dressed in a white robe sitting on the right side; and they were alarmed. But he said to them, "Do not be alarmed. You are looking for Jesus the Nazarene, who was crucified. He has been raised! He is not here. Look, there is the place where they laid him. But go, tell his disciples, even Peter, that he is going ahead of you into Galilee. You will see him there, just as he told you." Then they went out and ran from the tomb, for terror and bewilderment had seized them. And they said nothing to anyone, because they were afraid.

—Mark 16:1–8 NET

With fear—that's how the Gospel of Mark ends, which shouldn't be all that surprising. After all, even in first-century

Palestine, dead people were not known to stand up, discard their burial robes, and take a casual jaunt down to Galilee. That's the stuff of ghost stories, the kind of tale one hears when huddled around a campfire late at night or watching an episode of *The Walking Dead*. Yet the earliest of the Gospel narratives concludes on a note of sheer terror: "And they said nothing to anyone, because they were afraid." For a religious document, it doesn't have a very comforting way of bringing things to a close. But the Gospel of Mark isn't meant to comfort, nor is it a mere religious text. It is something altogether different. It's a horror story.

Even if it's not immediately obvious, contemporary horror stories are animated by a similar kind of aesthetic vision. And while this aesthetic impulse can be identified on both formal and folk levels, it is most fully embodied by concrete cultural artifacts—stories about upside-down worlds filled with empty tombs and the walking dead. It is for this reason that an aesthetic account of a cultural artifact like *Stranger Things* illuminates important dimensions of contemporary atheism that might otherwise go unseen and unsaid. The horror genre thus serves as a unique instance in which philosophical a/theism finds material expression. But the aesthetics of a/theism is more than a hermeneutical lens by which to analyze and interpret a cultural production like *Stranger Things* (although this is surely one of its key contributions). It also opens up a reading of otherwise "sacred" texts like the Gospel of Mark.

To approach the Markan narrative through the lens of the aesthetics of a/theism is not to read it as an authoritative religious text, but rather to read the Gospel as an actual horror story and, in the process, to see what emerges.[1] In other words, it's not about how or whether the philosophical constructs of atheism line up with (or fail to line up with) orthodox interpretations of Scripture. Instead, it's about exploring the ways in which the aesthetic dimensions of a/theism might shed new light on the contours, textures, and overarching structures of Mark's Gospel narrative. Given the chance, a/theism (as evidenced by the poetic structures of a show like *Stranger Things*) reveals something hidden within the Gospel story that is otherwise out of reach theologically and, in so doing, serves as an invaluable resource for engaging in theological conversations in a post-secular context.

It's a Strange, Strange World

Horror stories are perhaps best known (and enjoyed) for their ability to provoke a visceral sense of surprise or fright. But the first and most significant way in which horror fiction expresses the aesthetic dimensions of a/theism is through its depiction of an encounter with the unhuman "world-without-us," or what Rudolf Otto calls the "numinous." For instance, every element of the *Stranger Things* narrative has to do in some way with a confrontation between two different orders of the real: the world as it exists for humankind and the unthought, unhuman, nonconsensual world that refuses to play by human rules. Mike, Dustin, Lucas, and Eleven name this realm of radical otherness the "Upside Down" in part because they intuitively recognize it as a negation of the world in which they live and move and have their being, an inversion of what humans presume to be the normative, right-side-up world.

The same can be said of the terrifying creature that emerges through the portal where these two worlds meet. Much like the Upside Down, it can be understood only in terms of what it isn't—what isn't known and can't be said about it. Anthropomorphic language fails. It isn't that its face is something like a human's, only slightly distorted. It's that it has no face at all. It is fundamentally unhuman. Therefore, when this unhuman creature from a world-not-for-us comes (no)-face-to-face with humans, they respond with equal parts fear and awe. The ensuing chaos and violence they encounter certainly amplify their overwhelming sense of terror. But at the very same time, the dawning realization that the whole of reality may not actually be for them also evokes a sense of amazed wonder. In some form or fashion, all of the principal characters become fascinated—possibly obsessed—with the Upside Down, seeking to know more about it through science (Dr. Brenner) or myth making (Dustin, Mike, Lucas, and Eleven) or direct experience (Joyce and Hopper), even as they remain uneasy with its radical unknowableness. In other words, when confronted with the numinous other, characters and audience alike become awestruck and terrified by the very real possibility that humanity may not be the hub around which reality turns.

A second way in which *Stranger Things* manifests the aesthetics of a/theism has to do with the show's depiction of the

Upside Down world-without-us as neither absolutely transcendent nor wholly immanent, but as suspended in a kind of immanent transcendence. In the story world of *Stranger Things*, the Upside Down is neither above nor below the right-side-up world, as if it were a kind of heaven or hell or even purgatory. But neither is it subsumed within material reality. It is something else altogether. Thus, echoing what Joyce Byers and Hopper both verbalize at different points in season 1, neither the both/and schema of modern science (according to Hopper) nor the either/or schema of religion (according to Joyce) are able to make any meaningful sense of the trauma that haunts their lived experience. On a purely pragmatic level, neither of these logics works. The only thing that does work is the logic of neither/nor.

In this way, both Hopper and Joyce operate according to a kind of cosmic pessimism, not because they are prone to despondency and despair, but because it is the only viable alternative to what they perceive as the truly nihilistic pursuits of religion and science. And they aren't the only ones. For instance, when trying to make sense of the mysterious realm in which their friend Will Byers is trapped, Mike, Dustin, and Lucas find their science teacher's explanations either inadequate or irrelevant. Neither do they find religion to be of any help. In fact, they don't even consider it. Instead, they opt for the *D&D Expert Rule Book*, drawing upon popular culture as the authoritative resource for understanding their situation in greater depth and, by extension, determining how best to respond. In other words, for this group of adolescents, it becomes clear that neither scientific laws nor therapeutic religion offer satisfying accounts of the category-shattering phenomena they have observed and encountered. Where reason and religion seem to fail, the poetics of material culture prevail.

Third and finally, *Stranger Things* embodies the aesthetics of a/theism because its starting point is the catastrophic. It presents a narrative world that not only is haunted by past horrors and present traumas but also portends future losses and lost futures. Represented best by the sound of a mysterious creature that remains just beyond the camera's frame, this catastrophic presence is both inside and outside the show's visual images as its absent center. It is that which is present even (and perhaps especially) in its absence. As such, it can only be expressed aesthetically—through formal categories that traffic in the paradoxical, like the sound-image dynamic of audiovisual media.

The same goes for another catastrophic force that also pervades the narrative world of *Stranger Things*: love. Indeed, the upending, reinventive, world-changing presence of love in *Stranger Things* doesn't merely reinforce or illustrate the conceptual schemata of philosophical atheism. Instead, it actually broadens the horizons of what might be possible, especially as it relates to the ways in which the human imagination figures forth the world in the midst of a seemingly endless slate of horrors.[2]

However, the self-giving love demonstrated by the characters in *Stranger Things* is something that can be neither represented nor comprehended in any straightforward sense, because at its most basic, the aim of love is to experience the world from the point of view of difference—from the standpoint of the other. In this way, love's logic is rightly understood as para-logical, because while it doesn't operate according to syllogistic reasoning, it isn't *illogical* either. Rather, it is fundamentally interstitial and liminal. It construes difference not as oppositional, but as a relational dynamic that constitutes the structure and substance of all reality. Love is thus a virtual reality that simply cannot be captured propositionally or arithmetically. It exceeds the limits of one's rational capacities. In fact, sometimes, as in the moments when Joyce Byers can *feel* the presence of her missing and purportedly dead son through blinking Christmas lights, it doesn't make any logical sense at all. Or to quote Sheriff Hopper's assistant, Flo, again: "Only love makes you that crazy, sweetheart, and that damned stupid."

Flo's witty aphorism underscores the core dilemma that *Stranger Things* presents both to its characters and its audience. The show's suggestion that love might be the deepest of all catastrophes—one that both exposes the limits of the human and serves as humanity's only hope—is indeed an absurdity. Love is too weak, too fragile, too fleeting to be an adequate response to life's horrors. It almost sounds crazy. No, it *is* crazy. Either love is irrational, or—as Joyce Byers eventually discovers—the world is not as everyone imagines it to be. Few thoughts, if any, could be more terrifying.[3]

The Horror of Disguising Disgust (Mark 16:1–2)

The final chapter of Mark's Gospel ends on a similarly terrifying note to the one sounded by *Stranger Things*. In the wake of his crucifixion, Jesus's disciples are caught up in a radical kind of uncertainty. The only thing of which the disciples can be certain is that the world is not what they thought it was—not by a long shot. That being said, after the disciples have observed the Sabbath like the faithful Jews they are, a small cadre of them approach the tomb. Significantly, it is a group entirely comprising women. The men are nowhere to be found. Like the female protagonists of *Stranger Things* (Eleven, Joyce Byers, and Nancy Wheeler), these women demonstrate a level of courage and commitment that their male counterparts simply do not possess (although the males in *Stranger Things* are nowhere near as craven as Jesus's male disciples). Just like that, the catastrophe of Jesus's death has already upended the status quo, already overturned the world as it was thought to be.

Undaunted, these three faithful women bring "aromatic spices" (Mark 16:1) to the tomb in order to anoint their beloved teacher's body. This surely has to do with some manner of religious observance, but the ritual significance of this burial practice in no way diminishes the fact that the act of anointing a rotting corpse with aromatic spices also functions instrumentally as a way of disguising its horrid smell. An illuminating parallel is found in the account of Jesus raising his friend Lazarus from the dead. In that story, found only in John's Gospel, Lazarus's sister Martha begs Jesus not to have the stone rolled away from the tomb's entrance because her brother had already been inside for four days and "by this time the body will have a bad smell" (John 11:39). Jesus responds not by addressing her concerns about unearthing a potentially offensive odor, but by speaking of the "glory" of God (John 11:40) manifesting itself in and through her sibling's rotting flesh. According to Jesus, this divine glory—this decidedly unhuman reality—was about to reveal itself as hidden within the concrete particularities of decomposing matter. What is more, given his refusal even to acknowledge Martha's worries, the possibility that a putrid smell might emerge from Lazarus's tomb seems to be completely beside the point to Jesus. Revulsion is to be expected. It's what happens when the unhuman domain of God's glory impinges upon the world of flesh and blood. In fact, disgust is apparently such a common response to the meeting of these two worlds that, from Jesus's perspective, it simply goes without saying.

In this way, the tomb itself becomes a site where the enigmatic world-without-us intersects with the visibly perceptible world-for-us, and this holds true whether the decaying corpse belongs to Lazarus or Jesus. To use the language Jesus most often employs in Mark's Gospel, the kingdom of God makes itself known at these burial sites, revealing itself not as some absolute, transcendent reality, but as the unhuman world breaking into the human world. And the primary reason everyone knows this is clearly the case is that the whole thing just reeks. It's a smell that generates a sense of disgust because it is, in fact, disgusting—revolting even.

Lest anyone forget, Mark is telling a horror story. So of course the women need to bring aromatic spices with them to Jesus's tomb, not simply to observe some ancient burial practice or to show their respects, but because strange and unsettling side effects are par for the course when the unhuman intrudes into the human realm. In other words, what's terrifying about Mark's Gospel narrative is not all the death and dying (that's just sad). It's not even that, for a moment, the disciples (and the readers) think they may have gotten Jesus entirely wrong. What's truly terrifying is that, at the site of Jesus's burial and resurrection, humanity encounters, perhaps for the very first time, the unhuman world-without-us. To be sure, it's a somewhat provocative claim. But more importantly, it's one that is made possible only by allowing the aesthetics of a/theism to take the lead.

The Horror of the Nonconsensual (Mark 16:3–4)

Obviously, given both the smell and the threat of ritual impurity that open tombs present, the stones that cover them are not lightweight, nor are they easily moved. So the women are immediately faced with the question of how they are going to anoint a body they cannot access. Knowing that a potential plot hole of this sort might take the reader completely out of the story, the author of Mark inserts a line of dialogue in the form of a rhetorical question: "Who will roll away the stone from the entrance to the tomb?" (v. 3). This is a deft storytelling move—one that has numerous modern equivalents. For instance, among screenwriters for film, it is fairly common knowledge that, if some element of a script involves an event that could potentially undermine the internal logic of a film's narrative world, the best way to prevent the audience from questioning the credibility of the entire movie is simply to place their concerns in the mouth of an on-screen character. Hearing someone call out the impossibility or absurdity of the situation gives viewers permission to suspend their disbelief, for the storyteller acknowledges the anxiety that the narrative inconsistency creates. It's a way of preparing the audience for what's to come, inviting them to embrace the fantastic or fabulous elements of a story, rather than dismiss them out of hand.

In addition to its rhetorical power, the brief conversation that takes place between the women also serves to underscore Mark's larger narrative goal. More specifically, in Mark's story world, there are unseen forces in play—powers and principalities that are not even remotely human. Indeed, when the women arrive at the tomb, the first thing they notice is that "the stone, which was very large, had been rolled back" (v. 4). Neither the women nor readers know by whom, or in what way, or to what end. No one seems to know, and no one is ever told. Like the women at the tomb, readers can only suspend their disbelief. But the implication is clear: whoever or whatever moved the stone away isn't playing by the rules of this world. The mover of the stone doesn't seek out consent from anyone before defying the laws of physics.

Without any apparent concern for the humans who may or may not be involved, a stone too heavy for this small handful of women to budge has been rolled back by we know not what. Rather than a clumsy plot device, the stone now serves as circumstantial (and thus ever more mysterious) evidence of that which is not only unseen but unthinkable and, most likely, entirely unhuman. As in all good horror stories, it's something that thickens the plot.

The Horror from Below (Mark 16:5)

Unlike the other two Synoptic Gospels, both of which tell multiple stories of transcendent beings appearing and striking fear in the hearts of those to whom they communicate, Mark contains no such accounts. Whereas Luke's narrative notes that "two men . . . in dazzling attire" (Luke 24:4) were at the tomb and Matthew's account states that the women were met by "an angel of the Lord descending from heaven . . . [whose] appearance was like lightning, and his clothes were white as snow" (Matt 28:2–3), in Mark's version there is only a "young man dressed in a white robe" inside the tomb, "sitting on the right side" (Mark 16:5).

Again, nothing is known about who or what this young man is, but in Mark's narrative, he is decidedly less ethereal—less angelic—than in the other Gospel accounts. He's more grounded, literally so (i.e., he's sitting on the ground), and the details provided about him are concrete and particular ("young," "in a white robe," "sitting on the right side"). This characterization prompts readers to assume a much different posture toward the narrative events—almost the opposite of the shepherds in Luke's story, who were left staring up into the empty sky after the angels departed. Instead, in a move that mirrors the camera's descent in the establishing sequence of *Stranger Things* (i.e., from the night sky to the catastrophic ground below), the author of Mark focuses the reader's attention downward, as if to suggest that one's primary point of reference for understanding the catastrophe of Jesus's death is not somewhere out there or up there, but on the ground, in the muck and mire of a now-empty tomb.

The Horror of Going Down the Rabbit Hole (Mark 16:6a)

Nonetheless, it isn't long before even the ground gives way. Indeed, at this point in the narrative, three days have already passed since everything in the women's lives has been upended, yet they have no idea just how unthinkable their world is about to become. As the young man greets the women, he tells them not to be alarmed, a comforting gesture if not for the fact that the entire scenario unfolding before them is completely alien and, as a result, completely terrifying. He then outlines a series of facts they already know, almost as if he were carefully reorienting someone returning to wakefulness after being unconscious for a time: "You are looking for Jesus the Nazarene, who was crucified" (v. 6). This is an obvious, redundant statement. The *kata-strophe* (the over-turning) started with Jesus's crucifixion—of this the women are already well aware. Yet little did they know, up until that very moment, that they had only been peering over the brink of an expansive abyss. It isn't until the young man delivers his next line that they become aware of their precarious position and, just as suddenly, plunge over the edge: "He [i.e., Jesus] has been raised!" (v. 6).

It's not incidental that, in the Acts of the Apostles, one of the chief accusations brought against followers of the Way is that they are guilty of overturning the social, political, and cultural orders of the day. Their very way of being "turns the world upside down" (Acts 17:6). The Greek word used here is *anastatoo*, which shares the same root as *anistemi*, to "resurrect" or to "raise up from the dead." In other words, just as the young man inside the tomb knew full well, resurrection is nothing if not catastrophic; it quite literally turns the world Upside Down.

And this is precisely where Mark's Gospel not only finds a home in the horror genre but also is best understood in these terms. Like all good horror stories, Mark's Gospel dares to suggest that to live in light of resurrection is not to await some disembodied utopia. Rather, it is to embrace a catastrophic relation toward the world. It is to submit oneself to the normative power of the Upside Down—the world-without-us that, while always hidden and elusive, exposes the limits of human comprehension, not to mention the sheer hubris of humanity's thoroughgoing anthropocentrism.

The Horror of Neither Here nor There (Mark 16:6b–7)

For the small group of women who went to the tomb that day with the intention of anointing a dead body, it was likely difficult to discern which of the young man's claims were based in some kind of reality (e.g., Jesus's body is gone) and which, if any, were simply the ravings of a well-dressed lunatic (e.g., Jesus has risen). Of course, it was early in the morning and they hadn't slept in days, so perhaps they could assume they were suffering from a series of post-traumatic stressors that had triggered some kind of mass hallucination. Indeed, it would be perfectly reasonable to conclude that this was all taking place in their heads. But that would also mean their own senses were no longer reliable. And in truth, the alternative explanation is no less disturbing. That is, it might *not* be a hallucination. It might have really happened. Jesus might have actually turned the world upside down. If that were the case, their sanity would not be in question, but they would be forced to admit that reality itself was no longer intelligible. Either way, here they are, listening to an enigmatic young man sitting inside a tomb suggesting that Jesus has "gone ahead of them." He is neither "where they laid him" (v. 6) nor yet in Galilee (v. 7). The strange young man assures them, however, that they will be able to see Jesus at some point in the future, just as he once told them.

Again, none of this is comforting, much less rational, but it certainly makes for a psychologically haunting and viscerally compelling story. The vacillation between these two types of radical uncertainty is the very thing that marks out the terrain of the horror genre. Indeed, as some have said, "everything interesting happens in the middle."[4] And this is precisely why Mark's narrative is not only riveting but also deeply disturbing, for it doesn't operate according to the logics of both/ and or either/or. It isn't that Jesus is either a dead and rotting corpse or a disembodied spirit hovering above and beyond the world. Nor is it that Jesus is both dead (in actual fact) and alive (in the spirit of the community). In Mark's Gospel story, it's neither/nor. The empty tomb signifies neither the absolute absence of a transcendent God nor the indiscriminant presence of an immanent God, but the emergence of an immanent transcendence.

Like the *acousmêtre*—that terrifying character in horror fiction whose acoustic presence underscores the absence of the images we see—Jesus is present in the tomb only as its absent center.[5] Or to put it somewhat differently, in Mark's Gospel, the empty tomb includes but does not incorporate something that can be neither represented nor comprehended, namely, a world turned Upside Down—a world resurrected.

The Horror of the Numinous (Mark 16:8)

In response, these women do what most reasonable people would do. They run as fast as they can. Despite the young man's attempts to set their minds at ease, the women simply turn around and flee. What is more, they don't utter a word about what they have seen and heard—not to anyone. Instead, they run in silence "because they were afraid" (v. 8). Theirs isn't a generic sense of fearfulness, nor is it even a specific fear of something as quotidian as death. After all, they went to the tomb prepared for, and even expecting to face, death. Rather, what frightened these women was their encounter with the unknown and unknowable otherness of the world. They ran not from death, but from that which they had no capacity to comprehend. They ran from the world-without-us.

A more straightforward reading of Mark might interpret both the women's fear and their refusal to tell anyone about the missing body as having to do with the politics of the situation, as if they fled the burial site to avoid the same fate as the Nazarene who had been executed as a political dissident just days before. But the text moves in a decidedly different direction, revealing exactly why they run. It's because "terror and bewilderment had seized them" (v. 8). Even though the language is Greek, this pairing of "terror" (Gk. *tromos*, or "tremors") with "bewilderment" (Gk. *ekstasis*, or "amazement, awe") is nearly identical to Otto's conceptualization of the *mysterium tremendum et fascinans*. This means that Mark's Gospel ends in an unsettling way: not with the blessed assurance of a risen Christ but with a pervading sense of both wonder and horror. The disciples were fearful, yes. But they were also seized by something truly amazing, something truly awe-ful: the numinous.

These final moments of raw and unfiltered fear, of being seized by "terror and bewilderment," can mean only one thing. Mark's narrative is in fact a piece of horror fiction. Indeed, the Gospel of Mark can and should be read as a horror story, not because evil spirits haunt its narrative world (although they do), nor because it manages to generate a visceral sense of dread among its readers (although it does), but because horror is the only appropriate response to an encounter with the numinous—the wholly other that is at one and the same time intoxicatingly attractive and unapproachably terrifying.

The Horror of Humility

All told, if the true horror of the empty tomb is that it occasions an encounter with the world-not-for-us, then a fundamental reworking of what it means to be a person of faith is in order. Above all else, it would seem that theists in general and Christians in particular are in need of a more humble imagination. Humans are not the center of any universe—neither the known nor the unknown. In fact, the distance between humanity's understanding of the world-for-us and the world-without-us is so gaping that it would be far more helpful (and more accurate) to speak of that which cannot be known and cannot be said and cannot be thought.

To assume a more humble theological posture is not to embrace an easygoing skepticism or cynicism, nor is it to abandon theological commitments. Instead, it is to acknowledge that no encounter with the world-without-us is necessarily or automatically positive. It is always to enter a cloud of unknowing, to walk a *via negativa*, to come face-to-face with no-thing. It is to inhabit a space where the resurrection is always held in abeyance, always to come, always going ahead of us as the presence of an absence. And in truth, this is to claim little more than what Christian mystics and negative theologians like Meister Eckhart and Teresa of Ávila have long suggested. But it also finds an analogue in the work of some of the more prominent theological figures of the twentieth century.[6]

Nevertheless, reading the Gospel of Mark as a horror story invites a far more radical (and potentially catastrophic) kind of theological humility—one that moves beyond a mere passing acknowledgment of the limits of human language. Put baldly, an encounter with the unhuman suggests that God's project in the world is ultimately not "for" human persons.

As the women at the tomb discovered, to think this thought (or unthought) is not only terrifying, but also profoundly humbling. It fundamentally upends, relocates, and relativizes the anthropocentric models that so often monopolize theological reflection. Theodicy, for instance, simply has no place in this paradigm shift. However much humans might want the universe to be morally coherent, and however much they might even be justified in railing against its seemingly amoral structure, the whole notion of theodicy turns on the assumption that the plight of humanity bears some kind of ultimacy. But it doesn't. When viewed from the perspective of the world-without-us, humanity can only ever be a penultimate concern. Rather than quasi-heterodox, this notion is, in fact, profoundly theological and biblical. Just ask Job.[7]

That being said, the inclusion of the character of Peter in Mark's narrative remains instructive. While delivering his message to the women at the tomb, the young man calls out Peter in particular: "But go, tell his disciples, even Peter, that he is going ahead of you into Galilee" (v. 7). In the preceding chapters of Mark's narrative, Peter—thought to have been the most committed of all the disciples—vehemently denies Jesus the moment he encounters a potential threat to his own well-being. In the grand scope of Jesus's own confrontation with the unhuman, Peter's equivocations seem hardly worth mentioning. And yet, in Mark's account, it matters. Peter matters because, for Jesus, the world-for-us is meaningful, too, even if only penultimately.

Therein lies the scandal—the perverse core—of the Christian faith. Jesus isn't a detached observer of the human world, riddled as it is by horrendous evil. In the incarnation, crucifixion, and resurrection, Jesus himself participates in those horrors in order to address the non-optimal state of the human condition and the fractured relationship between the divine and the human.[8] To participate in the human condition in this way is to reach out to it—to attend to it—in love. It's a humbling and humiliating kind of love. It is self-emptying through and through (cf. Phil 2:7). It's personal, too. It's directed toward particular people like Peter who are hopelessly flawed. It's a love that demonstrates the catastrophic consequences of the unhuman world-without-us breaking into the world-for-us. When it does, it relativizes every human project, reflecting how penultimate each and every activity, anxiety, and experience of horror really is.

Like Peter, humans matter, but not ultimately. This is more than a humbling thought. For many if not most people living in late-modern society, it's an unthinkable thought. It's also downright terrifying. After all, much like the disciples, contemporary readers have just now come to realize that the tomb in which they stand really is empty. God is not there. Neither is God in some other, more fanciful place. In the presence of this divine absence, terror and amazement have seized them. They are also rendered mute. They dare say nothing to anyone, for they are afraid—so very afraid. And given the god-awful smell, they are probably pretty disgusted, too.

Notes

1. We want to make clear that we have no intention of entering into conversation with modern biblical scholarship or the history of biblical exegesis. These critical discourses are valuable in their own right, but engaging them here would, in important respects, defeat the purpose of reading Mark as horror fiction.

2. "The imagination is the activity through which the figures that pattern the data of experience emerge, are modified, and dissolve. Insofar as every figure presupposes the process of figuring, it includes as a condition of its own possibility something that cannot be figured. In a manner reminiscent of the torsion of thought through which we are able to think the unthinkable conceptually, figures 'include' but do not incorporate something that can be neither represented nor comprehended. Figures, therefore, are always disfigured *as if* from within." Mark C. Taylor, *After God* (Chicago: University of Chicago Press, 2007), 307 (emphasis in original).

3. In other words, "as with the horror genre itself," contemporary people find themselves "caught between two abysses, neither of which are comforting or particularly reassuring. Either I do not know the world, or I do not know myself." Eugene Thacker, *Tentacles Longer Than Night*, Horror of Philosophy 3 (Washington, DC: Zero, 2015), 6.

4. "Everything interesting happens in the middle, in the wavering between these two poles—a familiar reality that is untenable, and an

acknowledged reality that is impossible." Thacker, *Tentacles Longer Than Night*, 5–6.

5. Or, to use Taylor's somewhat more theological language, "The Incarnation is the negation of the radically transcendent God, and the Crucifixion is the negation of the isolated individual deemed divine. The Resurrection represents the double negation that issues in the sublation of opposites in a relation of identity-in-difference and difference-in-identity." Taylor, *After God*, 160.

6. Expanding upon Robert Scharlemann's work, B. Keith Putt offers an insightful exploration of the similarities and differences in the ways that Barth and Tillich name God in their respective theologies. As the title suggests, Barth labeled God the "no to nothing," while Tillich symbolized God as "nothing to know." See B. Keith Putt, "The No to Nothing, and the Nothing to Know: Immanent Transcendence as Eschatological Mystery," *Religions* 8, no. 64 (April 2017).

7. Marilyn McCord Adams suggests as much in her systematic Christology. For McCord Adams, God's unitive project is ultimately about God's purposes, and only penultimately (but still importantly) oriented toward the non-optimal situation in which humanity finds itself. "Personal intimacy with us is penultimate within God's unitive aims, and a main benefit of the Incarnation is that it enables God to meet us on our level." Marilyn McCord Adams, *Christ and Horrors: The Coherence of Christology* (New York: Cambridge University Press, 2006), 51.

8. McCord Adams, *Christ and Horrors*, 29.

PART II

The What

4

An Art Form: Music

"They told us our gods would outlive us / But they lied."[1] These may be the words of an aging musician, but it's hard to imagine a more fitting way to describe the underlying catastrophe that constitutes contemporary life. Written by Nick Cave, rock music's "Prince of Darkness," these lyrics also resonate quite remarkably with the concept of the "world-not-for-us." Indeed, the horror genre and certain forms of popular music are kindred spirits of sorts, tethered together by an aesthetic sensibility that is thoroughly a/theistic. The key difference between the two is that, whereas the horror genre maps out the location in which contemporary life unfolds (the where), popular music confronts listeners with the traumatic reality of life in a godless world (the what). Viewers might be able to close their eyes or turn away from the terrifying visions of televised horror, but no one has ear-lids with which to close their ears. In fact, for those who are able to hear, sound, like death, is inescapable.

Just as they do in the haunted world of *Stranger Things*, the aesthetic dimensions of a/theism manifest themselves most fully in and through concrete cultural artifacts like popular music, which is why the immense catalogs of creativity produced by Nick Cave, David Bowie, and Leonard Cohen are particularly important. One of most striking features of their collective body of work is that, throughout their careers, each utilized biblical imagery, scriptural references, and religious symbolism in his music. Yet none of them lay claim to any kind of formal religious belief. Rejecting the artificial binary between atheism and theism from the start, their music presents listeners with an alternative: to engage theology by intentionally avoiding the theological. This kind of a/theistic sensibility serves as the common chord that reverberates throughout their aesthetic productions and their personal and professional lives. Interestingly enough, it plays on unabated in their deaths, too, resonating in ways that perhaps even they would not have anticipated.

One More Time with Feeling

"Life is not a story, it's often one event piled on top of another event," declares Nick Cave in the lovely and poignant documentary *One More Time with Feeling*, released to promote *Skeleton Tree*, Cave's new album with his band the Bad Seeds.[2] In the wake of the tragic death of his fifteen-year-old son, Arthur, the documentary was Cave's idea, intended as a buffer, a way of promoting new work without having to face the press and the public.

To make an album and a documentary in the wake of immense grief and loss is, of course, an extraordinary accomplishment, although very early in the film, Cave wonders out loud whether or not the whole venture was a really bad idea. Thankfully, it's a truly extraordinary work. The accidental death of a child cannot be seen as anything other than monumental pain. But these two works are more than just admirable efforts at confronting life's tragic curveballs; they are perhaps the most honest and beautiful confrontations with grief to have come along in a long, long while. Along with David Bowie's final album, *Black Star*, which was loaded with meditations on what turned out to be the singer's own death, pop music in 2016 offered rich materials with which to face mortality through works resonant with deep honesty that offer no easy answers to life's challenges.

One might think that a film shot in the wake of such an immense tragedy would be voyeuristically morbid, but nothing could be further from the truth. *One More Time with Feeling* isn't heavy-handed or otherwise leaden. It just breathes and aches, and viewers breathe and ache with it. The film hints at Arthur's death from the beginning, but viewers are drawn deeper and deeper into the film before the tragedy is named. Filming in 3D might seem like a somewhat gratuitous choice for a documentary about recording a few songs, but the camera spirals through everything, gently drawing viewers into the heart of the matter. As it turns out, the special effect here is the very life of Cave's community, working through a torment difficult to imagine yet making something come to life in its wake.

What the film really does—and this might just be its greatest gift—is face grief in all of its rawness without making any attempt to fix it. Much like Christopher Hitchens challenging the notion of "fighting cancer," Cave faces the loss of his son not by crying out to God or overcoming the demon of loss and emerging triumphantly as the conqueror of grief. Instead, with candor, honesty, and deep pain, Cave acknowledges that there are events in life that bring about changes from which there is no recovery. "Time has become elastic," he says. "We stretch away from the event, but we are always snapped back to that moment when our life changed."[3] The challenge, then, and the gift Cave offers is to remind his listeners and viewers that surviving such loss is about figuring out, again and again, how to live with the unknown person the event has turned them into.

Seven of the eight songs featured in the film and in *Skeleton Tree* were recorded before the death of Cave's son, but they are not named. What remains is a work of art that offers up a meditation on the tragic unfairness of life. Death, it would seem, interrupts life, unconcerned as it is with the feeble little projects humans pursue. Toward the end of the documentary, each person featured in the film is shown portrait-like against a gray wall—the film crew, the band, Nick's wife, his surviving twin son, Earl, and an empty frame—the portrait of a missing son. Cave draws the segment to a close with his own voice-over narration, explaining that he and his wife have decided to be happy as an act of revenge.

One More Time with Feeling establishes the "what" of contemporary life. Reality itself is constituted by the traumatic. It is shot through with death. What is more, there is no longer any god to make sense of it all, which makes it all the more ironic that the only available resources for grappling with life's traumas are religious. Artists like Cave are attempting to navigate this chaotic and meaningless existence in and through the aesthetics of a/theism. When tragedy strikes, one must find a way to live again—without answers, because there are none. If this is the case, then Cave's path of happiness-as-revenge might just be the way to go, and music may be the only means anyone has for moving forward.

Nick Cave

Death has always been close to the surface in Nick Cave's work. In many ways, his career thus far has been shaped by death. The sudden death of his father when he was a teenager propelled him into music as a means of expiating the pain of that loss. More recently, the death of his young son, quite strangely and unexpectedly, served as a catalyst for his career, so much so that after more than three decades in the music business, he launched his first-ever arena tour in 2017. Without being insensitive, the growth in his popularity seems to be directly linked to the saddest moments of his life, and his authentic, confessional, and honest response to it.

Cave is an Australian-born singer-songwriter whose early

career began with a band called the Birthday Party. The Birthday Party was a punk band that was difficult to listen to. It had a small cult following that barely scratched the surface of pop cultural awareness except for the most exploratory of music fans. From there, Cave formed a new band, the Bad Seeds, which, in spite of a revolving group of musicians, continues to this day. Their output consists of sixteen studio albums, four live albums, two compilation albums, thirty-one singles, and five video albums. Among this potentially overwhelming surfeit of music, a few songs in particular—"The Mercy Seat," "Stagger Lee," and "Into My Arms"—are emblematic of the two interrelated themes that recur throughout Cave's larger body of work: love and death.

"The Mercy Seat"

"The Mercy Seat," written by Cave and Bad Seeds band member Mick Harvey, was released in 1988 on an album entitled *Tender Prey*. "The Mercy Seat" is a fan favorite that still elicits excitement from audiences every time it is performed. The song tells the story of a man about to be executed by the electric chair. The "mercy seat" refers both to the cover of the ark of the covenant, which created the space upon which Yahweh would appear to the people of Israel, and to the modern-day electric chair. Beyond the title, the song itself is loaded with religious allusions, employing both Old and New Testament references, but the vision of the mercy seat is what constitutes the core of the song: "And the mercy seat is waiting. . . . And in a way I'm yearning / To be done with all this measuring of proof."[4]

The more-than-seven-minute song revisits the chorus over fifteen times, and with each return, it builds upon the tension inherent in a man who is facing death yet, in the closing stanzas of the chorus, declares that he is "not afraid to die." With each refrain, the man moves ever closer to death. First his head and then the seat burns. It smokes and melts while his blood boils. The lyrics allude to the book of Leviticus and its tales of the spilling of blood on the mercy seat while the smoke of incense rises to the nostrils of God. And in Cave's vision, all of this is connected to the law of bloodguilt: an eye for an eye.

It's not an easy listen, in part because there seem to be two separate vocal intentions in the song. On the one hand, the lyrics are barely discernible at times, set against a background of a simple but defiant piano, piercing stabs of feedback, and guitar and drum samples that drive the song ever more frantically toward its crescendo. On the other hand, the song also plays with its lyric structure. At different points, the lyrics to what initially seem to be verses are sung over the same chord structure as the chorus, adding even more of a sense of chaos to the song. Still, some of the lyrics can be heard: "I hear stories from the chamber / How Christ was born into a manger / And like some ragged stranger / Died upon the cross."[5] Here, the Old Testament mercy seat, the manger, the cross, the throne of Christ, and the electric chair all collide into one apocalyptic image of redemption, injustice, and salvation.

It's one thing to read the lyrics and admire the giftedness of their author, but during a live performance, the song becomes something more than the sum total of its lyric poetry. Pop music creates meaning through the marriage of instruments as well as vocals. In fact, what a song means has as much to do with the emotional journey that it takes the listener on as with the content of its lyrics, and "Mercy Seat" is quite a journey. Replete with biblical imagery, it is a song of absence or emptiness, a song that questions the nature of reality, given God's notable absence in the midst of life's devastating injustices.

"Stagger Lee"

Another song that not only traffics in these kinds of theological paradoxes but also became a concert favorite for Cave devotees is "Stagger Lee," which came from the 1996 album, *Murder Ballads*. "Stagger Lee" is drawn from a popular American folk song about the murder of Billy Lyons by "Stag" Lee Shelton in St. Louis, Missouri, on Christmas 1895. As the story goes, Shelton and his acquaintance, William Lyons, are drinking in a saloon on Christmas night. Lyons, a member of St. Louis's underworld, is thought to be a political and business rival to Shelton. Possibly fueled by their consumption of liquor, the two men get into a heated dispute, during which Lyons takes Shelton's Stetson hat. Shelton then shoots Lyons, recovers his hat, and leaves the saloon. Shortly thereafter, Lyons dies of his injuries, and in 1897, Shelton is charged, tried, and convicted of the murder. He is pardoned in 1909, but returns to prison in 1911 for assault and robbery. He dies in incarceration in 1912.

The crime quickly entered American folklore and became the subject of numerous songs as well as folktales and toasts. The song's title comes from Shelton's nickname, Stag Lee or Stack Lee, which over time became Stagger Lee. The song was part of a series of new and traditional murder ballads, a genre of songs that relay the tales, details, and consequences of crimes of passion. Cave's version of Stagger Lee, laden with profanity, tells the story of his crime from a neutral position. He sets the tale in the 1930s with the opening line, "It was back in '32 when times were hard." In Cave's account, Lee calls himself a "bad motherfucker, don't you know / And I'll crawl over 50 good pussies just to get to one fat boy's asshole."[6] Quite intentionally, Cave layers obscenity after obscenity onto this tale of sex, violence, and ultimately, death.

Death carries the day in "Stagger Lee," and the graphic nature of Cave's lyrics certainly lends a sense of discomfort and dis-ease to all that transpires. In fact, one wonders how the song would be received (or rejected) if it were released today. Yet the larger point is that, whether Cave's songs are explicitly religious (like "The Mercy Seat") or not (like "Stagger Lee"), Cave's music effectively collapses overlapping binaries. In Cave's vision, there are no clear or distinct boundaries separating justice and injustice, sex and violence, love and death. "Stagger Lee" tells a story that takes place on Christmas—the day Christians celebrate the incarnation (i.e., divine embodiment)—but that story unfolds in an utterly profane world of sexual violence and bodily death. It thus confronts listeners with a kind of trauma that simply cannot be reconciled through easy answers born from a strict separation of theism and atheism. In Cave's mind, death simply deserves more credit than that.

"Into My Arms"

In stark contrast to the obscene profanity of a song like "Stagger Lee," the Bad Seeds released *The Boatman's Call* as their tenth studio album in 1997. The album is entirely piano based, a marked departure from the bulk of the band's earlier, post-punk catalog. It is a romantic yet sometimes somber album full of quiet. As such, *The Boatman's Call* remains one of the most acclaimed and beloved releases of Cave's career. Around the same time Cave entered this quieter period, he was also struggling to overcome a drug addiction. He gave a series of talks about music, which led to conversations about faith. He wrote an introduction for a special pocket-sized edition of the Gospel of Mark in which he discusses the safe and sanitized Jesus the church often advances—a tepid, placid figure who goes about patting children on their heads. This Jesus was of no interest to Cave, but another Jesus was: the lonely, isolated Jesus he found in the pages of the New Testament, particularly in the Gospel of Mark. As Cave matured and grew less and less fond of the fiery, apocalyptic imagery of the Old Testament, he sought a different muse for his creative process. At the time, Cave claimed that his creative imagination came from God—not the God of his childhood church, but the Jesus who railed against the establishment.[7]

When releasing *The Boatman's Call*, Cave described it as a non-metaphorical narrative of his own life, an autobiographical work centered on a relationship he knew would not last. In light of this personal revelation, the songs on the album seem to mine biblical imagery and religious practice more than any of his other works. As it grapples with theological tensions such as a personal lack of faith, individual sin, and the desire to do good, and as it explores more direct biblical allusions like the comforting hand of God and turning the other cheek, the album connects Cave's personal life with biblical imagery in a profound way. Given that the album is an exploration of a relationship destined not to last, which occurred at the end of the breakup of another romantic relationship, there is a sense in which the theological and the erotic come together in this piece for Cave. Once again, Cave's music rejects the easy binaries between the theological and a-theological, the sacred and profane and, in so doing, demonstrates how one might do theology not as an act of faith per se, but as an act of revenge.

When asked whether he considered *The Boatman's Call* to be any good, Cave replied that he really didn't care. He had made the album he wanted to make, one that was "slow from beginning to end, a slow, melancholic record, which is very sparse, very raw and beautiful."[8] The raw and beautiful nature of the album is apparent in one of its most beloved songs, which cannot really be called anything but a hymn. A gentle, piano-driven prayer, "Into My Arms" opens the album with the provocative lines "I don't believe in an interventionist God / but I know darling that you do."[9] It's a hymn to a lover, not the divine, but Cave uses the biblical imagery of an engaged and interventionist God as a foil against which the singer proclaims and declares his own love. Together, the music and lyrics suggest that, while the speaker does not believe in any kind of God who might have agency in the world, if he were to believe—if he were to offer up prayers and petitions—he would simply offer prayers on behalf of his love, asking that God send her into his arms. As a thoroughly humanist hymn, it ushers the listener into a collection of songs that continue to fuse the spiritual and the sensual, the sacred and the profane, the erotic and the contemplative, all the while using, as the press release that accompanied the album declared, "religious imagery to reflect the glory of personal love to affirm religious belief."[10]

The Boatman's Call anticipates and in many ways exemplifies Cave's decision to enact a kind of revenge by way of happiness. His primary response to the tragic dimensions of reality is a musical expression of belief—not in the divine, but in love and sex and death. His music assumes an aesthetic shape that leverages the power of theologically rich symbols even while it rejects those symbols on their face. In this way of engaging with the world, there simply is no room for either/or dualities. There is only religious imagery that celebrates human love and affirms religious belief.

David Bowie

David Bowie was like the Beatles were for an entire generation before him. He signaled a shift, a movement in the cosmos, a point of separation and departure from what had been. He was the perfect foil for life in the 1970s. Any giddiness left over from the sixties had dissipated, which meant that Bowie came to the fore just as social disillusionment gripped the United Kingdom along with the rest of the world. The swinging sixties gave way to the more sober and desperate seventies, and Bowie with his sound—the sound of dissonance, disconnection, and maybe even frustration—was just what listeners needed. He wasn't just playing music. He was inviting them to join him in a whole new world.

Bowie resisted and refused the dominant norms of existing society. The sixties might have advocated free love, but Bowie pushed for something else—a collapse of boundaries, a resisting of gender definition. He was queer before queer was a public idea. He played around with his sexuality, or at least gave the appearance of such, wearing dresses, using makeup, calling himself bisexual or pansexual or whatever else piqued his curiosity with regard to sex. Wrapped up in a homemade spacesuit or wearing theatrical feminine clothing and women's shoes, Bowie pushed the boundaries of what it meant to be male in 1970s Britain. His fans loved him for it, and he loved them back. He was the outsider, the alien, the man who fell to earth.

Of course, Bowie had influences, too, including his soul period, when he directly mined the rich heritage of black music. But he always added his unique twists, unexpected looks into a world not yet formed. Music lovers lapped it up. For thousands of fans locked up in the boredom of English life, wracked with confusion, angst, and a thirst for something more, Bowie told them they were not alone, that they were wonderful. It sounds trite, but it's true. He took his fans on a mind-blowing creative journey that lasted from the midseventies until his death in early 2016. Not all of his albums were great, but each was a revelation.

Needless to say, Bowie was not an artist prone to repetition. He had that late-modern restlessness so characteristic of those who live in a world unmoored from its past and uncertain of where it is ultimately headed. He put his restlessness into a ceaseless exploration of musical possibility, always pushing ahead, whether in favor or out of favor. He created any number of alter egos—Ziggy, the Thin White Duke, Major Tom, Aladdin Sane—all of them new incarnations of himself. He was a walking multiple personality, using characters to stake out new musical horizons.

If nothing else, Bowie's life and works demonstrate that religion is the most interesting where it is the least obvious. In a supposedly secular world, where religion has been swept aside in favor of other explanations of the nature of reality, and where the transcendent has been reduced to an occasional encounter, traces of the sacred appear in the most unexpected places, one of which is the music of David Bowie.[11] Not all of his music is obviously religious, and it is unlikely that many people would point to Bowie as an obvious ambassador for the divine, especially given the anti-clerical, anti-religious tendencies evinced in his music, interviews, and videos. In fact, at first blush, Bowie would seem to be a proponent of Nietzschean nihilism.

Yet one can trace in Bowie's music a faint sense of the divine in play. Notions about god are present and active from the start. That might be too strong of an assessment, so it may be more accurate to say that Bowie makes room in his music for a materialism that may or may not be infused with something more. For instance, he flirts with metaphysical conceptions at times: "I realize God is a young man too" is a line from one of the songs on his album *The Man Who Sold the World*.[12] At other times, Bowie's music, much like the music of Nick Cave or Leonard Cohen, holds a prayer-like quality. The prayers, if they can be called such, held within the structures of his songs have a desolate quality. Lamentation and yearning are their chief hallmark. Consider as well his duet with Annie Lennox at the Live Aid festival, where they sang the Lord's Prayer on behalf of a hungry African continent. Somehow, that prayer, out of all the things that could have been spoken, was the right one for him to offer up. It's not necessarily surprising when an artist birthed and bathed in Western civilization employs religious imagery and symbolism in his work. Still, there was David Bowie, leading a community of concertgoers in a sacred liturgy.

In a press release for his 2003 album *Reality*, Bowie states that he wanted to use this particular title and set it in capital letters to juxtapose an older understanding of the world with what he calls "the new tangle it's become."[13] He goes on to say that he was thinking about the notion that there is no ultimate reality anymore—that there are no absolutes left. According to Bowie, "This reality that we live through, its basis is more an all-pervasive influence of contingency rather than a defined structure of absolutes."[14]

This new world is the one that Bowie wanted to discuss in the early years of the new millennium, a world already ripped apart by 9/11, a world full of new entanglements and new complex realities. He believed contemporary people find themselves in a whole new world, a new reality, without the benefit of old gods to help them, because the old gods are dead, and humans have killed them. The resultant choices are to collapse in the face of this harsh new reality, to resurrect the old gods in the vain hope they might bring some measure of comfort, or to forge ahead into a new reality, trusting in the contingencies of life, rather than its guarantees.

So if Bowie has any religiosity, it is well hidden within the folds of his music. Glimpses appear sporadically here and there. However, it's nearly impossible to miss either his critique of religion or his use of biblical imagery to deliver this critique, which continued right up to his death. His album *Black Star*, released in 2016, is a meditation on mortality, death, and finitude. His last video was for the song "Lazarus," and in it he is strapped to a bed with strips of linen covering his eyes and buttons lying over his eye sockets like pennies. As Bowie/Lazarus is raised, the bed becomes upright as well, which makes it an explicit, albeit unsettling allusion to the

Lazarus tale. However, elsewhere in his work, what gets the most press is the critique of religion. Many of his videos feature him or other actors playing some kind of cleric, usually in some sort of moral compromise, as if to argue that true religion has been co-opted by the pretenders. In this way, Bowie assumes a quasi-prophetic role, reminding all those with ears to hear and eyes to see that the experience of the divine and the pathway to the sacred have been blocked by religious corruption.

Perhaps he is calling for reform, but it is highly unlikely that Bowie wanted to reestablish the role of traditional religion in society. Rather, in and through his music, he sought to expose the decadence of religion along with the emptiness of contemporary life—a life characterized by violence, rampant consumerism, and the perpetual pursuit of happiness, which create obstacles to a deeper engagement with reality (or REALITY). Bowie might not have called that which motivated him a spiritual desire, but that doesn't make it any less so.

In 2013, his album *The Next Day* appeared out of nowhere. Released on his sixty-sixth birthday without fanfare and without any inkling of its potential arrival, it was a marvelous feat in this age of digital leakage, where everything is seemingly known and promoted in advance. The first single is called "Where Are We Now?" It is surprisingly nostalgic for Bowie. In it, he reflects on his past and explores his own mortality—a mortality that none expected to come so quickly. In the video, Bowie is a "man lost in time," who is "walking the dead." It's a mournful song that springs into majestic and hopeful life when it is least expected. "Where are we now?" Bowie asks. It's a question reminiscent of Jesus, who frequently asked the Pharisees if they really had any idea what time it was (Matt 16:1–4; Luke 11:29–32; Mark 8:11–12). Asking these questions opens the door to a kind of theological reflection that offers something to a world struggling with new realities and old ghosts while also struggling to find a way into the future.

In 1999, Bowie was awarded an honorary doctorate from the Berklee College of Music and was invited to give the commencement address. During his speech, he told the graduates that he realized that authenticity was never going to be his strength, so he preferred thinking of music as a game of "what if?" This approach accounts for his amazing ability to bring together seemingly incongruous ideas and create something magical, something new, something that challenges the way things are and seemingly always have been. He also called himself a non-musician, saying that once he had gained enough competency to get his ideas across to other musicians, he had gone on a crusade to try to "change the kind of information that rock music contained." In doing so, he brought musical ideas from other genres into the heart of rock and roll and somehow made it all work. This creative energy continued right up to the very end when, on his sixty-ninth birthday, just days before his incredibly sad and untimely death, he released an album of new music called *Black Star*. In true Bowie fashion, it was backed by a group of jazz musicians with whom he had never recorded. It was a rock and roll album made by intentionally avoiding rock and roll.

Musicians like David Bowie serve as a reminder that people of faith (and theists in general) too often fail to recognize or simply refuse to take note of the changes in the cultural imagination. To acknowledge this fact is not to argue for hasty accommodations or spineless acquiescence to every perceived cultural pressure. However, all too often, the Christian community in particular seems incapable of rejecting what has become little more than an outdated and outmoded mythology—the myth of political power, cultural prominence, and ideological control. And that is indeed tragic. But Bowie can help.

Indeed, embedded within Bowie's music are a few best practices for engaging and responding to the various traumas that have come to define life in the twenty-first century—a set list of a/theological possibilities inspired by the least religious person in rock. Bowie's life and music encourage listeners not to operate with false binaries, but instead to practice "what if," to bring together incongruous pieces of information, to live with contingencies rather than chase absolutes, to find new conversation partners, and to engage theology by intentionally avoiding the theological. All of this is, of course, easier said than done, but at the very least, these practices name the what faced by many, if not most, contemporary people. And in a genuinely constructive sense, they also point people in the direction of the what if.

133

Leonard Cohen

Much like Bowie, the poet-theologian Leonard Cohen sadly left this earth all too early. All that remains is his disembodied voice. Cohen spent years sitting in silence in a Buddhist retreat center yet never considered himself a religious person. Known as both the Godfather of Gloom and the Grocer of Despair, Cohen did not start his music career until the age of thirty-two. He wrote eighty verses for his song "Hallelujah" while dressed in his underwear, banging his head on a hotel floor. In so doing, Cohen declared that both the perfect and the broken hallelujahs have equal value. His credo was "There is a crack in everything; that's how the light gets in." And he was right.

A Canadian-born poet and songwriter, Cohen passed away in 2016. He left behind a wealth of works in a number of genres, particularly poetry and music. He began life as a poet but transitioned to music when he realized that he would probably not be able to make a living out of writing poetry. His first album, *The Songs of Leonard Cohen*, was released in 1967, when he was thirty-three years old. He continued to make music until his death at eighty-two, releasing his final album shortly before his death.

Cohen's life involved various excursions into religion. He was Jewish but became a Buddhist convert later in life. He spent many years as a monk serving a Japanese Buddhist teacher in Southern California. Yet his increasing public popularity came through the recording of his music by other artists. When guitarist and singer Jeff Buckley released an angelic cover of an obscure Cohen song called "Hallelujah"—a song that Cohen's record company had initially rejected—it became one of the most covered songs in popular music history. Telling the story of David and Bathsheba, "Hallelujah" explores brokenness and failure, love and lust, and sexuality and spirituality. In multiple ways, it serves as an example of Cohen's amazing ability to take biblical imagery and deploy it in musical contexts to explore timeless themes of human yearning, loss, and desire. The song captures the struggle between basic human desires and the search for spiritual wisdom, the earthly and erotic versus otherworldly forms of sensuality. It's about being caught between those two places, a space that Cohen inhabits and returns to frequently in his songs. "Hallelujah" also exposes Cohen's ambivalence about God and religion: "Now maybe there's a God above / But all I ever learned from love / Is how to shoot at someone who outdrew you."[15]

The "maybe" is telling. It speaks both to Cohen's brutal honesty and his ability to capture the struggle many have with the whole idea of belief and surrendering to God. It took Cohen more than five years to write "Hallelujah," in large part because he had to whittle the song down from the eighty verses he wrote to the fifteen that remain in the full version of the song.

His final album bore the provocative title *You Want It Darker*. The first sound on the album is a choir from the Shaar Hashomayim Synagogue in which Cohen's family worshipped, intoning the Hebrew word *hineni* (here I am) over and over. The last sound is Cohen apparently addressing Jesus with a certain irrevocability: "It's over now / the water and the wine / . . . / I wish there was a treaty / between your love and mine."[16]

Judeo-Christian imagery runs throughout Cohen's work, and it is front and center on this album. Cohen's figure of Jesus has things to answer for. From Cohen's perspective, Jesus has let everyone down. "Vilified, crucified, in the human frame / A million candles burning for the help that never came" is Cohen's challenge to the God who has declared his presence in the song.[17] It's a startling piece of work that confronts a bland and naïve acceptance of God in the face of life's complexities. A surface reading of Cohen's lyrical content could lead to the mistaken conclusion that he is a true believer of the first order, when in fact he uses religious symbolism to address his concerns and ambivalence about religion and spirituality.

You Want It Darker is a menacing critique of God and religion, and the songs move from anger to a sort of resigned acceptance and back again. The heart of the album beats loudly and clearly in the opening track. It is a response to God that borders on the blasphemous: "If you are the dealer, I'm out of the game / If you are the healer I'm broken and lame."[18]

But this intense face-off with God is tempered by sparks of rapturous worship. On one occasion, as the choir drops out, Cohen fills the vocal silence with his own chanting, "*Hineni, hineni*"—a Hebrew cry of surrender and devotion, the reply of one who hears God's call and is ready to act. Cohen's music, which seems to reject religion outright, also seems to imply that there are other ways of being "religious" in the world.

In an interview with Jon Pareles in the *New York Times*, Cohen said, "I've always found theology a certain kind of delightful titillation. Theology or religious speculation bears the same relation to real experience as pornography does to lovemaking. They're not entirely unconnected. I mean, you can get turned on. One of the reasons that they're both powerful is that they ignore a lot of other material and they focus in on something very specific. In these days of overload, it's very restful to know, at last, what you're talking about."[19] Cohen is not theologizing here as much as he is using religious symbolism as a means to a different kind of end. His goal is not to proclaim God, but rather to challenge God in and through God's own words.

The lyrical interrogation continues with the next track on the album, "Treaty." On first listen, it sounds like a treaty, a love pact made between a man and a woman, but as the couplets continue to unfold, Cohen once again stands toe-to-toe with God, voicing his disappointment with the role God has played in human affairs: "I've seen you change water into wine / I've seen you change it back too," he almost sighs over a gentle piano melody. Expressing frustration at the lack of fulfillment his devotion has brought him, he finally concludes, "Only one of us was real and that was me."[20]

For a man who spent much of his life in the midst of a religious pursuit, the tone of resignation is weighty, yet at the very same time, it signals a delicate hopefulness. Cohen seems to acknowledge that God's claim upon his life and upon the world lacks authenticity. And yet—and yet he continues to lodge his complaint, to air his disenchantment, to voice his despair.

Cohen's critique continues in songs like "It Seemed the Better Way," which again hints at his disappointment in the figure of Christ. The hope found in that initial encounter with the divine has slowly given way to a frustration and a resignation that these metaphors and allegories and biblical ideas no longer deliver on their promises: "Now it's much too late / To turn the other cheek."[21]

In addition to distinctly a/theological musings like these, Cohen was also known for the ways in which his many sexual exploits found their way into his music. As "Hallelujah" clearly demonstrates, he managed to effortlessly blend the overtly sexual with the theological: "And remember when I moved in you / The holy dove was moving too / And every breath we drew was Hallelujah."[22] He also traded in a more obscure collapsing of the boundary between religious adoration and romantic love, an inclination exemplified in the song "If I Didn't Have Your Love."

All told, the critique of religion found in Cohen's deeply spiritual work is not merely the rejection of religion or theology, nor is it an embrace of radical atheism. It is instead an interrogation of the role and function of religion in our time. It is to question what, if anything, the religious impulse has to say to contemporary society and how spiritual desire might reveal itself if it were to do so today.

Cohen's work revolves around the dilemmas of material existence and the question of whether or not life is meaningful. He has said that he feels that religion is essentially the process of people gathering together to "articulate the burden of their predicament."[23] This sentiment is why his works seem to swing back and forth between devotion and rejection, between the sacred and the profane, even between theism and atheism. What he brings to his music are his own quandaries—moral, ethical, sexual, political—expressed in his deeply personal and wonderfully poetic manner. But they are also dilemmas that many if not most contemporary persons face. Unmoored from traditional answers and unsatisfied with religion's responses to the burden of existence, they must raise these questions again and in new ways. Cohen not only gives voice to these dilemmas, but also willingly lives in the mess and tension of them, accepting the basic paradox of human existence. Finally, Cohen's gift is his ability to wrap a deeply personal song in such a manner that anyone who has the ears to hear can identify with the ideas contained within it. As Cohen himself admits, "My work may not be always easy to understand, but it is easy to embrace."[24]

Leonard Cohen, David Bowie, Nick Cave—each of these artists approaches God and religion from a unique perspective, but what they have in common is a willingness to introduce religious or spiritual concepts into their music, sometimes overtly, sometimes implicitly. More importantly however, their long careers contain multiple references to the spiritual right alongside scathing critiques of religion. Cave deploys trenchant religious language to rail against the very god he rejects as a way of responding to his own trauma in a godless and thereby meaningless world. Bowie provides listeners with a way of doing theology that intentionally avoids the theological. Cohen's work is as devotional as it is sensual, leading listeners into questions surrounding material existence and spiritual longing. In other words, when taken together, their music functions neither as theistic nor atheistic, but as a rejection of the theist-atheist binary altogether. Although many may view these crudely as opposites, in the works of these musicians, theism and atheism are deeply intertwined.

It is impossible to understand the full depth and texture of this a/theistic vision without acknowledging its aesthetic dimensions. What's more, the aesthetic features that structure and support contemporary a/theism more broadly can be discerned only in and through material culture—concrete artifacts like the music of Cohen, Bowie, and Cave. The individual lives and musical catalogs of these three artists demonstrate an a/theistic sensibility that is at once holy and broken. Indeed, theirs is the kind of artistry that prompts everyone within earshot to sing "Hallelujah" to the god who is absent. God is dead. Praise God.

Notes

1. "Distant Sky," lyrics by Nick Cave, on *Skeleton Tree*, Bad Seed, 2016.

2. *One More Time with Feeling*, Iconoclast, 2016, DVD.

3. *One More Time with Feeling*.

4. "The Mercy Seat," lyrics by Nick Cave, on *Tender Prey*, Mute Records, 1998.

5. Cave, "The Mercy Seat."

6. "Stagger Lee," lyrics by Nick Cave, on *Murder Ballads*, Mute Records, 1996.

7. Roland Boer notes that two elements of Cave's life come together in this period, one taken from his songs, and the other from his interviews and writings. The first, according to Boer, is "the clear connection that Cave makes between the Bible and his autobiography." The second aspect, which is more intriguing to Boer, is that when his songs do invoke the Bible, "they do so not merely in an autobiographical fashion, but also with Christological focus." Roland Boer, *Nick Cave: A Study of Love, Death and Apocalypse* (Sheffield, UK: Equinox, 2012).

8. "Nick Cave, Alphabetically [1997] by Dave Thompson (Alternative Press)," Nick Cave Online, August 13, 2006, http://www.nickcave.com.

9. "Into My Arms," lyrics by Nick Cave, on *The Boatman's Call*, Mute Records, 1997.

10. "Old Nick," interview of Nick Cave by Simon Hattenstone, *The Guardian*, February 22, 2008, https://tinyurl.com/y6uvs89r.

11. We owe this insight to Mark C. Taylor, *Erring: A Postmodern A/theology* (Chicago: University of Chicago Press, 1984).

12. "The Width of a Circle," lyrics by David Bowie, on *The Man Who Sold the World*, Mercury Records, 1970.

13. David Wild, "David Bowie's Reality," BowieWonderworld, 2003, https://tinyurl.com/ya7p72cc.

14. Wild, "David Bowie's Reality."

15. "Hallelujah," lyrics by Leonard Cohen, on *Various Positions*, Columbia, 1984.

16. "String Reprise/ Treaty," lyrics by Leonard Cohen, on *You Want It Darker*, Columbia, 2016.

17. "You Want It Darker," lyrics by Leonard Cohen, on *You Want It Darker*, Columbia, 2016.

18. Cohen, "You Want It Darker."

19. Jon Pareles, "At Lunch with Leonard Cohen: Philosophical Songwriter on a Wire," *New York Times*, October 11, 1995.

20. "Treaty," lyrics by Leonard Cohen, on *You Want It Darker*, Columbia, 2016.

21. "It Seemed the Better Way," lyrics by Leonard Cohen, on *You Want It Darker*, Columbia, 2016.

22. Cohen, "Hallelujah."

23. "In Conversation with Leonard Cohen," interview by Chris Douridas, KCRW Radio, October 22, 2016, https://tinyurl.com/yabuc4dr.

24. Douridas, "In Conversation with Leonard Cohen."

5

How Darkness Sounds

Nick Cave, David Bowie, and Leonard Cohen are almost but not quite thoroughgoing atheists. Their music is often bathed in what can only be called the profane. Nevertheless, they all have extensive bodies of work filled with religious symbolism, theological musings, and both critiques and affirmations of the pursuit of the sacred. There's the post-punk primal scream of Cave's railings against the world, against love, against God; the polished, futuristic strivings of Bowie, whose music challenged conventional notions about life, God, identity, and politics; and the more poetic musings of Leonard Cohen, whose lyrical explorations of erotic, carnal love are set in the biblical landscape of his Jewish upbringing. Yet none of them claims a firm belief in God or religion per se.

That statement may come as a surprise to some, particularly for fans of Leonard Cohen, whose life was marked by a deep commitment to spiritual practices. Shortly before he died,

Cohen was interviewed by Chris Douridas of KCRW public radio, along with a group of music reporters from around the globe. Douridas asked Cohen about the influence of religion in his life, and he replied:

> I've never really considered myself a religious person; I don't have any kind of spiritual strategy. I limp along like so many of us do in these realms. Occasionally I've felt the grace of another presence in my life, but I can't build any kind of structure on that. So I feel that this is a vocabulary that I grew up with. This biblical landscape is familiar to me, and it's natural that I use those landmarks as references. Once they were universal references, and everybody understood and knew them and could locate them. That is not the case today, but it's still my landscape. I try to make those references. I try to make sure they are not too obscure. Beyond that I dare not claim anything in the spiritual realm for my own.[1]

Mining a musical landscape similar to Cohen's, Nick Cave's creative output also is filled with christological imaginings, rants against the Divine, and at times, a humble embrace of God. Images and ideas taken directly from the pages of Scripture enliven his music. His songs are both confessional and brutally honest. Like Cohen, Cave uses romantic and erotic love (of a more overtly sexual and profane type) as the foil against which these theological images are cast. But as with Cohen, Cave lays no claim to personal religious belief, although he has taken more than one position on this throughout his life. In 1998, he declared in a lecture on poetry in Vienna that "the actualizing of God through the medium of the love song remains my prime motivation as an artist."[2] That very same year, in a newspaper interview, he also said that he had "a passing, skeptical kind of interest [in religion].

I'm a hammer-and-nails kind of guy."[3] And in *One More Time with Feeling*, he explained that his personal involvement with religion was essentially tied to his drug addiction. He went to church on his way to visit his drug dealer as a way of trying to settle an inner behavioral code. Beyond that, he declared, "God exists in my songs, but not in my life."[4]

Cohen and Cave's ambivalence notwithstanding, David Bowie is probably the most elusive and enigmatic figure among the three. Bowie made a career out of shape shifting, creating persona after persona to serve his musical muse. His comments and public statements often mirrored the character he was playing at the time. He is on record as having tried a wide array of spiritual practices and religious traditions, from Tibetan Buddhism to Christianity, as well as Satanism and Nietzschean philosophy. In 2003, he declared in his own humorous way, "I'm not quite an atheist and it worries me. There's that little bit that holds on: Well, I'm almost an atheist. Give me a couple of months."[5]

The Incredible Need to Believe

These three musician share similarities, of course, but they execute those similarities in their own unique, creative ways. They each make new revelations out of their profanation, and they all exist in a world constituted by the transgressive and the irreverent. The ancient myth of Orpheus helps reveal how music is particularly well suited for transgressing certain culturally embedded norms (religious or otherwise). According to legend, Orpheus, who had learned from Apollo how to play the lyre, was such a gifted musician and beautiful singer that he could charm wild animals and cause trees to uproot and follow after him. Jason took him on his quest for the Golden Fleece, and Orpheus saved Jason and his crew from shipwreck by drowning out the voices of the Sirens with his own music. He met and fell in love with the beautiful Eurydice, whom he decided to marry. At their wedding, Eurydice was set upon by a woodland creature. In her effort to escape the clutches of her attacker, Eurydice fell into a nest of vipers, suffering a fatal bite on her heel.

Her body was discovered by Orpheus, who, overcome with grief, played such a sad and mournful song that every creature and all the gods wept. On the gods' advice, Orpheus traveled to the underworld to meet with Hades. Once there, he played his lyre and sang his song. His music softened the heart of Hades, who agreed to allow Eurydice to return to earth on one condition: Orpheus had to walk in front of her and not look back until they both reached the upper world. He set off with Eurydice following closely behind. Perhaps because of his anxiety, as soon as he reached the upper world, he turned to look at her, forgetting that both needed to be in the upper world before he did. As a result, Eurydice vanished back into the underworld forever. Orpheus then retreated from human contact and spent his days singing to nature and the beasts of creation.

The Orpheus myth suggests that music can move listeners, capture and guide their imagination, and even create spaces where meaning can be made. But music doesn't merely move people emotionally and create interior spaces where meaning can be formed: music is the very medium through which humans discover the knowledge the gods seek to impart. The figure of Orpheus is therefore a "theologian *par excellence*, . . . the interpreter of the gods."[6]

There has long been a sense that music, that most pervasive of human creative acts, somehow connects humanity to the divine, however that term is understood. It does not mean, nor does it have to mean, that music is sacred in a traditionally religious sense or that music is a medium for the exploration of particular religious notions. It's much broader than that. To say that music connects humanity to the divine suggests that, whatever else happens in music, something about it creates an inward space for a kind of openness to something other, something more, something beyond the material. Put differently, music guides listeners as they cross boundaries. And Orpheus is the archetypal boundary-crossing figure, the one who creates community through his art, who creates emotional spaces in which new meaning and new ideas can be traded and exchanged, and who can move the listener to heights of ecstasy or the depths of despair.

It is hard to imagine that one so determined to get his love back—one willing to venture into the unknown underworld, where few, if any, dared to venture—would fail to heed the single condition that would grant him the desire of his heart. Yet that is exactly what Orpheus did. Just as Cave, Bowie, and Cohen do, Orpheus transgresses. He refuses to stay within the boundaries set by the gods of the underworld.

In the first place, he crosses between worlds. The material and the ethereal, the world above and the world below, the world of light and the world of darkness—each of these dualisms sets the stage for the boundary-crossing power of music. But Orpheus also affirms the essentially transgressive nature of music itself. Even if it is innocuous in a formal sense, music is always performed in a contested space and, as a result, cannot help but perforate artificial boundaries established by those who benefit from clearly drawn distinctions.[7]

This notion sheds some light on how to approach the work of these artists. They, and their work, exist in the contested spaces of late-modern society, which speaks both to their apparent ambivalence toward religion and their employment of religious symbols and ideas as a means to describe their lives. In a post-theistic world, faith is hard to come by. But as Julia Kristeva has noted in her book *This Incredible Need to Believe*, the need to believe is a pre-religious human impulse, something that resides within every person.[8] There is a desire to explore what it means to be human, to find some shape to existence—to discover meaning, even if this meaning-making process is primarily about coming to terms with the meaninglessness of existence. Kristeva elsewhere articulates the unique tension of the time in which contemporary persons are caught—a tension between the need to believe and what she terms the desire to know.[9] The need to believe is the pre-religious quest for meaning, but this need is lived out in tension with the desire to know, which is characterized by a science- and rationalism-supported quest for knowledge about the world. She argues that this is a unique context that demands a reconfiguring of both religion and secular humanism.

Kristeva goes on to make the somewhat startling observation that the current climate of religious upheavals, outbreaks of radicalized violence, and the apparent clash between numerous ideologies are simply surface issues. The real and more challenging dynamic is what she calls the rift or void that "separates those who want to know that God is unconscious and those who would rather not know this."[10] The notion of an unconscious God is found in the writings of French philosopher Jacques Lacan, who said that the "true formula of atheism is not god is dead . . . but that god is unconscious."[11] Lacan means that even if someone consciously denies a belief in God, their actions demonstrate an unconscious belief in such a being or, at the very least, in a similar kind of ordering principle for life. Similarly, Slavoj Žižek has suggested that the paradoxical situation of modern life is that, in spite of what appears to be a pervasive rejection of God, many if not most people still seem to act as if God exists, because they have not freed themselves from life's prohibitions.[12] When people can no longer look to the church for help or guidance in these matters, they create their own mechanisms both to limit and to liberate themselves.

The mood of a/theism, its aesthetic impulse, inhabits and, in important respects, is made possible by this fraught and fractured space. It's why, in the transgressive space in which art and creativity operate, a rejection of god does not result in the abandonment of religious symbolism or even the dismissal of divine prohibitions. For even if the creators and consumers of art no longer have faith in God, they must continue to believe in human destiny and creative possibility. In the mind of Kristeva and others like her, this fundamentally human pursuit is accomplished not by abandoning the Christian tradition, but through the reclamation of Christianity's openness to self-questioning and its search for knowledge.

Cave, Cohen, and Bowie each navigate the tension inherent in this kind of self-questioning in and through their musical productions. In so doing, they provide listeners with the aesthetic resources necessary for engaging in any pursuit that involves both the need to believe and the desire to know. Their music thus establishes a new set of coordinates for navigating the contemporary landscape, marked as it is by the death of the death of god.

Creative A/theism: Nick Cave

For Nick Cave, belief in God may not exist outside of his music, and Christ may only be present as a muse for his explorations of love. Nevertheless, he leaves space for some kind of sacred conversation in and through his art. Cave's uncertainty about the reality of the divine is pervasive. The opening line of his song "Into My Arms," which declares his lack of belief in an interventionist God, encapsulates one of the recurring themes in his lyrical work. For instance, in the song "Oh My Lord," he intones: "The ladders of life that we scale merrily / move mysteriously around / so that when you think you're climbing up / in fact you're climbing down."[13]

In these lyrics, Cave demonstrates his uncertainty about the realm of the sacred, even as he seeks ways to live differently within the material order. For Cave, the modern world is an unfriendly place filled with people who "ain't no good." Whether it's the self-righteous moralists of "God Is in the House" or the murderous thugs, pimps, and whores of his *Murder Ballad* album (whose title refers to a genre of songs that describe crimes of passion), the desolate world of Cave's creative imagination almost exclusively comprises depraved human characters in all their gory detail. The figures that dot the landscape of his song-worlds are almost hyperreal, cartoon-like versions of reality, whether it's the ego-inflated pimp who is Stagger Lee or the strange creatures, human and otherwise (such as a kitten with bear claws and a crazed girl gnawing her knuckles), in the song "Where Do We Go Now but Nowhere?" This exaggerated vision of a doomed, crazed, and apocalyptic world is at once a creation of Cave's imagination and a commentary on the actual world gone wrong—a world driven by greed, religious prejudice, injustice, murder, and a dearth of erotic love. For Cave, the world is marked by misery and despair. It is a sort of hell on earth that sits in the shadow of a largely disinterested God who has much to answer for.

Cave's creativity doesn't merely exist in this kind of theologically conflicted context; it thrives here. It is perhaps best summed up in the song "Darker with the Day," in which the main character goes to church to seek for God, but finds no help: "Inside I sat, seeking the presence of a God / I searched through the pictures in a leather-bound book / Found . . . a gilled Jesus shivering on a fisherman's hook."[14]

This is not what the seeker was hoping to find, but things are not much better outside in the world—a world filled with "amateurs, dilettantes, hacks, cowboys, clones."[15]

Part of Cave's appeal is his dark view of life. Through words and sounds, he turns over the stones and exposes the dirt that lies beneath the surface of culture's dreams of redemption. For Cave, the remedy is not a return to God, nor will romantic love solve humanity's dilemmas. The pursuit of erotic desire and romantic love are, arguably, the principal aim and context of his theological musings, but these, too, are marred by sorrow and, at times, bitterness.

Beyond romantic love and religious devotion, Cave advocates for an embrace of creativity. Indeed, in a 1997 interview, he claimed that creativity allowed him to keep God alive. In Cave's theology, Christ is the Lord of creativity. For instance, in his introduction to the Gospel of Mark, Cave presents his vision of Christ. He speaks of Christ's essential humanness, his isolation, and his anger. He claims that Christ was a victim of "humanity's lack of imagination" and was crucified with the "nails of creative vapidity."[16] For Cave, to follow Christ—to be Christlike—is to defy mediocrity and embrace the creative life.

Cave's commitment to, and faith in, creativity as a means of redemption or salvation carries a great deal of currency in a post-religious, post-secular, post-theistic world. Just as his music suggests, creativity is the pathway out of boring jobs, desperate lives, and a world without the gods. It thus serves as the first coordinate for navigating reality in the wake of god's death.

Deworlding A/theism: David Bowie

Like the mythic boundary crosser Orpheus, David Bowie made a living crossing boundaries. More specifically, Bowie was the consummate trickster—a man who began life as Davy Jones, only to become David Bowie, Ziggy Stardust, Major Tom, Aladdin Sane, the Thin White Duke, Halloween Jack, and more. He was the singer-songwriter who became an experiential rock musician, employing Dada and Surrealist games to create his music. He was the rock star whose body became a site for the exploration of gender, sexuality, and technology. He was the heterosexual musician who wore dresses and makeup and created gender-bending characters. He continually traversed boundaries and, in so doing, offered his followers permission to transgress the conventional norms of society and discover their inner Ziggy, their multiple personalities, their own way in a world gone wrong. He was also the man who challenged society by wearing high heels and for forty years creating music that defied categorization.

One of the major theological challenges in the twenty-first century is the loss of the self, the shift from the idea of the stable self to a sense that the self is mutable and malleable. Or at least that's the claim that Mark I. Wallace makes in *Fragments of the Spirit.*[17] The mutable self is a central element of David Bowie's work. Through his creation of ever-changing public selves, he carves out a space in which listeners might not only express who they are (or are becoming), but also navigate the ever-changing world in which they live. Put differently, music like Bowie's permits "a kind of deworlding of the world," an experience in which a particular mood or emotion tells the listener that the world is not in agreement with the self.[18] Indeed, a deworlding impulse motivates much of Bowie's artistry. His songs about life, the world, and the world of the self invite listeners to disrupt their normal, mundane lives and establish a new order of being, a new way of being themselves.

Where Cave and Cohen explore the transcendent in their work, Bowie explores the immanent, material world. While his music traffics in religious imagery on occasion—and he certainly explored aspects of religion and spirituality in his personal life that found their way into his music—the philosophical nihilism of Nietzsche most profoundly shaped his output. In particular, his early albums—*The Man Who Sold the World*, *Hunky Dory,* and *Ziggy Stardust and the Spiders from Mars*—are full of Nietzschean philosophical concepts. The social discontent Bowie names in much of his music becomes a site for reframing many of the themes that were central to Nietzsche's work. Bowie weds a Nietzschean nihilism with his own rejection of a world of conformity to norms and values that no longer fit the times. For Bowie and Nietzsche before him, social codes inhibit the very liberation of spirit and freethinking they claim to protect.

Bowie's views about the state of affairs in contemporary life are perhaps best seen in one of his more popular songs. "Life on Mars" asks the very direct and simple question: Is there life on Mars? It is, of course, a question to which there is not yet an answer, but this is precisely Bowie's point. There are certain things that humans simply do not, and perhaps cannot, know, and this inability to know generates a great deal of anxiety and fear. Given these severe epistemological limitations, Nietzsche believed that the role of art and the artist was not merely to reflect life as it is presented, but rather to create life actively. This culminates in his idea of the "will to power," the notion that human beings must take responsibility for their choices and then act. Each individual, according to Nietzsche, bears the responsibility alone for the choices they make, and in this way can create a life that is meaningful and beautiful. This decidedly Nietzschean perspective on creating a meaningful life permeates Bowie's artistry. Or as Critchley put it, "At the core of Bowie's music is the exhilaration of an experience of nothing and the attempt to hold on to it."[19] Holding on to nothing seems paradoxical, but it is emblematic of Bowie's musical world.

Whether or not one concludes that Bowie's attempt to "hold on to nothing" makes him a thoroughgoing nihilist might very well depend on whether or not one's view of nihilism is negative or positive.[20] Nihilism is often viewed as a fairly negative and pessimistic outlook, leading only to pointlessness and despair. But in fact, nihilism is not the same thing as pessimism. Far from it. Rather, it is the belief that all values are equally baseless and that nothing can be known (which is why it should not be confused with optimism either). Nietzsche argues that the effects of a nihilistic outlook would eventually destroy all metaphysical, religious, and moral convictions and precipitate a profound crisis. But for Nietzsche, whose writings on art and creativity reveal a man very much committed to joy in life, the impending crisis isn't cause for despair or despondency. Nor is it the end of the world. It is only the beginning.

When Nietzsche proclaimed the death of God, he named the death of a particular God—a metaphysical God who provides the transcendent point of reference for the moral ordering of the cosmos. And while this death heralded the end of God, it was not the end of the world. Rather, the proclamation of the death of God was a way of saying that the Western world could no longer believe in a divinely ordained moral order, and that this turn from belief would lead to a rejection of belief in objective and universal laws, and that this loss of an absolute basis for morality would lead to nihilism. Nietzsche believed that nihilism was a means of revisiting the foundation of human values and discovering values deeper than the Judeo-Christian values he declared dead and gone.

The Nietzschean concept of the death of God is central to Bowie's creative ethos and is also the key to understanding the aesthetics of a/theism. The rejection of the old gods, the old conventions, and the old social codes is not simple rebellion. It describes the mood (the aesthetic shape) of the times, which is why Bowie's music serves as a second coordinate for sojourners attempting to navigate a restless world in the process of reconfiguring itself.

Sensual A/theism: Leonard Cohen

In 2009, Leonard Cohen released his first book of poetry since 1984. Along with a few song lyrics, it contains 167 poems that explore themes ranging from the nature of the self, to eroticism, to death. Many of them were written while he was living at a Zen monastery in Mount Baldy, California. Cohen titled the volume *The Book of Longing*, an apt title for a man whose work has been characterized by longing from the moment he began writing poetry decades ago.

Leonard Cohen spent most of his artistic life exploring the dark places of human experience. The book is named after the first poem, which focuses on the main themes of Cohen's larger body of work: desire, depression, and absence.

> I followed the course
> From chaos to art
> I'm living on pills
> For which I thank G-d
>
> My page was too white
> My ink was too thin
> The day wouldn't write
> What the night penciled in[21]

The core desires about which Cohen sings extend to the very depth of the human self. In fact, he once stated in an interview, "Not having a self is what we all most passionately desire. We desire it in love; we desire it in food; we desire it visually in sunsets. We want to give ourselves to experience, and when you give yourself to an experience, you have no self, and that's why it feels good."[22] Through songs that deal with love, sex, and spirituality, Cohen seeks to capture something of that desire and the sensation of giving oneself to an experience. His music is largely internal and addresses the turmoil of those caught in the throes of both desire and depression.

Cohen's music speaks to those for whom the "promise and indeed necessity of external political, social and cultural change has always been secondary to, or problematized by, the existential, internal, subjective struggle to survive."[23] The struggle to survive, to overcome desire, to fulfill desire, and to deal with absence and the depression that it brings is what Cohen seeks to achieve in his work.

God is often so present in much of Cohen's writing that assumptions about his spiritual life have long been seen as integral to understanding his work. But in spite of his use of biblical imagery and various theological constructs, Cohen remains painfully aware that God is experienced more often as an absence than a presence in his own life and the lives of others. Cohen won't find any answers by turning to God, not because these answers can be found elsewhere, but because they do not exist. And everyone—believers and nonbelievers alike—must come to terms with that reality. The goal is to invoke God not as a panacea, but as a device for thinking about how to handle a world without God. Says Cohen, "One idea on my new record [*The Future*] is that the human predicament has no solution. . . . We were tossed out of the garden; this isn't paradise. And to look for perfect solutions is a very difficult burden to bear. That's my theme: it's a mess—thank God."[24]

The journalist Edward Docx describes Cohen as the John Donne to Bob Dylan's Shakespeare.[25] The difference between Cohen and Donne might be that, while both explore ideas about the spiritual and the sensual, romantic love and God, for Cohen, love and God are one and the same. According to Cohen's artistic vision, love can bring everything together: sex, relationships, religion, politics, spirituality, metaphysics, and even the tormented human soul that feels itself torn by competing desires, aching loss, and existential sadness. Indeed, as Cohen says, "Love is the only engine of survival." Here, then, is the third and final coordinate.

The A/theistic Piety of Pop Music

The transgressive world of music that Cave, Bowie, and Cohen inhabit is a world of darkness and challenge (i.e., the what), a world tossed about by the loss of values, the loss of meaning, and the loss of God. In this liminal, transgressive space, the three musicians attempt the process of rethinking and reframing what it means to be human, to live after the death of God in a post-theistic, a/theistic world where material reality is infused with a need to believe and impaired by a desire to know. In other words, their music does not simply describe what it is that contemporary persons face, but following Michel Deguy, it also makes "revelation anew out of profanation," refiguring and revivifying the relics of tradition. Their music is not "a simple refusal of faith," and it is most certainly not a "rationally over-confident refutation of its reality either."[26] Rather it is a suspension of belief in favor of a new way of being in the world. It is a reframing of binaries and a refusal to capitulate to old codes that no longer hold the definitive clues to how people should live. It is a resolutely a/theistic piety with its feet firmly planted on the earth.

Embodied as it is in these concrete forms, the aesthetic shape of Cohen's, Cave's, and Bowie's music sheds light on various dimensions of contemporary atheism that would otherwise remain inaccessible. Chief among others is their clear and discernible call to love. In this way, the a/theism these musicians embrace is neither a negation (of theism) nor a loss (of faith), but the very means by which they earnestly, faithfully, and constructively engage the tumultuous world they inhabit (i.e., the what).

Notes

1. "In Conversation with Leonard Cohen," interview by Chris Douridas, KCRW Radio, October 22, 2016, https://tinyurl.com/yabuc4dr.
2. Robert Eaglestone, "From Mutiny to Calling upon the Author: Cave's Religion," in *Cultural Seeds: Essays on the Work of Nick Cave*, ed. Tanya Dalziell and Karen Welberry (New York: Routledge, 2016), 143.

3. Thomas Bartlett, "The Resurrection of Nick Cave," *Salon*, November 18, 2004, https://tinyurl.com/ya2t3wyu.

4. *One More Time with Feeling*, Iconoclast, 2016, DVD.

5. "I'm Not Quite an Atheist, and It Worries Me," interview of David Bowie by Anthony DeCurtis, *BeliefNet*, June 8, 2005, https://tinyurl.com/y9mwr8ub.

6. E. T. A. Hoffmann, quoted in Christopher Partridge, *The Lyre of Orpheus: Popular Music, the Sacred, and the Profane* (New York: Oxford University Press, 2014), 1 (emphasis in original).

7. Music, as Partridge notes, "may articulate faith, hope and love in largely innocuous and mundane ways, but it often, though not always, tends to do this from within the contested spaces of the modern world." Partridge, *The Lyre of Orpheus*, 5.

8. Julia Kristeva, *This Incredible Need to Believe* (New York: Columbia University Press, 2009).

9. Kristeva, *This Incredible Need to Believe*.

10. Kristeva, *This Incredible Need to Believe*, 26.

11. Jacques Lacan, *The Seminar*, book 11, *The Four Fundamental Concepts of Psychoanalysis*, trans. Alan Sheridan (London: Hogarth Press / Institute of Psycho-Analysis, 1977), 59.

12. Slavoj Žižek, "Hidden Prohibitions and the Pleasure Principle," https://tinyurl.com/y7lb8jav.

13. "Oh My Lord," lyrics by Nick Cave, on *No More Shall We Part*, Mute, 2001.

14. "Darker with the Day," lyrics by Nick Cave, on *No More Shall We Part*, Mute, 2001.

15. Cave, "Darker with the Day."

16. Nick Cave, "Introduction," in *The Gospel According to Mark* (Edinburgh: Canongate, 1998).

17. Mark I. Wallace, *Fragments of the Spirit: Nature, Violence, and the Renewal of Creation* (London: Bloomsbury T&T Clark, 2002).

18. According to Simon Critchley, music like Bowie's "is not a way of somehow recalling human beings affectively to a kind of pre-established harmony with the world. . . . [Rather], Bowie permits a kind of deworlding of the world." Critchley, *Bowie* (New York: OR Books, 2016), 38.

19. Critchley, *Bowie*, 63.

20. Indeed, this is one of Critchley's main observations about Bowie's music.

21. Leonard Cohen, *The Book of Longing* (New York: HarperCollins, 2006), 1.

22. "Leonard Cohen on Poetry, Music and Why He Left the Zen Monastery," interview by Terry Gross, *Fresh Air*, National Public Radio, October 21, 2016.

23. Peter Billingham, *Spirituality and Desire in Leonard Cohen's Songs and Poems* (Cambridge: Cambridge Scholars Publishing, 2017), 4.

24. Leonard Cohen, quoted in David Browne, "Leonard Cohen's 1993 Interview: Why the Singer Was the Next Best Thing to God," *Entertainment Weekly*, November 11, 2016, https://tinyurl.com/ydats9ms.

25. Edward Docx, "Leonard Cohen Is John Donne to Bob Dylan's Shakespeare," *The Guardian*, November 19, 2016, https://tinyurl.com/zelolru.

26. Michel Deguy, *A Man of Little Faith*, trans. Christopher Elson (Albany: State University of New York Press, 2014).

6

The Cry on the Cross as God's Apostasy

They brought Jesus to a place called Golgotha (which is translated, "Place of the Skull"). They offered him wine mixed with myrrh, but he did not take it. Then they crucified him and divided his clothes, throwing dice for them, to decide what each would take. It was nine o'clock in the morning when they crucified him. The inscription of the charge against him read, "The king of the Jews." And they crucified two outlaws with him, one on his right and one on his left. Those who passed by defamed him, shaking their heads and saying, "Aha! You who can destroy the temple and rebuild it in three days, save yourself and come down from the cross!" In the same way even the chief priests—together with the experts in the law—were mocking him among themselves: "He saved others, but he cannot save himself! Let the Christ, the king of Israel, come down from the cross now, that we may see and believe!" Those who were crucified with him also spoke abusively to him.

Now when it was noon, darkness came over the whole land until three in the afternoon. Around three o'clock Jesus cried out with a loud voice, "Eloi, Eloi, lema sabachthani?" which means, "My God, my God, why have you forsaken me?" When some of the bystanders heard it they said, "Listen, he is calling for Elijah!" Then someone ran, filled a sponge with sour wine, put it on a stick, and gave it to him to drink, saying, "Leave him alone! Let's see if Elijah will come to take him down!" But Jesus cried out with a loud voice and breathed his last. And the temple curtain was torn in two, from top to bottom. Now when the centurion, who stood in front of him, saw how he died, he said, "Truly this man was God's Son!" There were also women, watching from a distance. Among them were Mary Magdalene, and Mary the mother of James the younger and of Joses, and Salome. When he was in Galilee, they had followed him and given him support. Many other women who had come up with him to Jerusalem were there too.

—Mark 15:22–41 NET

It's difficult to imagine two words more dangerous than *what if*, especially for religious folks. It's also difficult to imagine a more transgressive artist in recent memory than David Bowie—a musician whose life and work provide a compelling lens through which to read against the grain of just about any story, even a sacred one. So when it comes to the Gospel of Mark, to approach the narrative with Bowie's question of "what if?" in mind is to engage in a kind of thought experiment. It's an imaginative excursion animated by the joining together of what seem at first blush to be two incongruous artifacts (i.e., sacred texts and profane art). It is neither the development of a biblical theology nor a theological interpretation of Scripture. Rather, to bring Bowie's question of "what if?" to bear on an otherwise revered text is to engage in a thoroughly a/theistic exegesis—an interpretative move that many are likely to resist precisely because of the text's sacred status.

Moreover, to ask "what if?" is not simply a matter of playfully reimagining the Gospel narrative. Instead, like all deconstructive projects, this form of interrogation strikes at the very structures of belief that uphold the contemporary imagination—traditions of interpretation that, in their ossification, have become more unassailable and sacrosanct than the sacred texts themselves. Some may be surprised to discover that Mark's narrative actually invites this kind of reading. Still, to ask "what if?" of the Gospel is, in actual fact, to ask probing questions of longstanding interpretive traditions, and that can be a dangerous business indeed. Jesus asked "what if?"; look where it got him.

It may be for this very reason that Nick Cave, Leonard Cohen, and David Bowie each in his own way demonstrates a kind of ambivalent obsession with the subversive preacher from Nazareth. It may also be why their collective body of work so helpfully illuminates both the Gospel narrative as a whole and, even more specifically, Jesus's cry on the cross in Mark 15:22–41. When we approach the sacred text with the work of these musicians in mind, a number of insights emerge that speak directly to the mood of the a/theistic age that has now dawned.

Asking "What If?"

What if? What if the cross were a kind of divine *memento mori*—a concrete reminder of God's own mortality? Jesus was, after all, brought to Golgotha, otherwise known as the "Place of the Skull" (v. 22), and skulls have long functioned as aesthetic objects meant to encourage reflection on the brevity of existence.[1] But the cross is also both more and different than that. If it truly is a *memento mori*, then the cross is a work of art that signals not just the death of god, but also the apostasy of god. It is symbolic of that moment (however fleeting it might have been) when God became an atheist.

On the surface, it's an absurd premise. God cannot logically apostatize against God, which is why the crucifixion story is best understood not as tragedy, but as a kind of tragicomedy. Indeed, the actions of the various characters who feature prominently in Mark's crucifixion scene verge on the satirical. In a kind of inversion of the book of Jonah, when even the livestock of Nineveh repent in sackcloth and ashes (Jonah 3:8), it seems that the whole of the created order—both human and nonhuman—stops in its tracks to denounce the man from Nazareth, mocking his very existence.

It all starts with the divvying up of Jesus's possessions, which effectively reduces the crucified to a commodity (v. 24). At the same time, the brutally efficient system of capital punishment (crucifixions start promptly at nine in the morning!) carried out by the Roman military appears to mock him (v. 25). In addition, the nation-state openly smears him by referencing his supposed "kingship" (v. 26). And if all that weren't bad enough, as he hangs between two legitimately convicted criminals, justice itself turns its back on him (v. 27).

But it gets worse. The masses defame him, too, taking just enough time out of their busy schedules to use his own words against him (vv. 29–30). The religious leaders also pile on, reminding him of the blasphemy they found so threatening (v. 31). Finally, even those who are being crucified along with him join the fray, somehow mustering enough energy to hurl insults toward him in the midst of their own torturous deaths (v. 32).

It's enough to make one wonder where God is in all of this. Eli Wiesel overheard a similar question in the midst of a Nazi concentration camp, where he witnessed a young child being hanged. His reply: "Where is He? Here He is—He is hanging here on this gallows."[2] Without question, Wiesel presents a haunting image. But in Mark, there aren't any gallows; there is only gallows humor. It's all just so over the top. Quite literally, everyone takes a turn defaming Jesus, which suggests that, wherever God may be, God most certainly isn't hanging on the cross with Jesus. Besides, that's too idealized—too romantic. The real truth is that, along with everyone and everything else, God also has forsaken Jesus. God is throwing dice with the executioners, utterly indifferent to the naked man dangling above their heads.

If this is indeed the case, then Leonard Cohen had it right about Mark's Gospel account all along: "You Want It Darker." This is dark comedy at its finest and at its darkest. Indeed, it begs for a reconsideration of the closing segment of Monty Python's *Life of Brian*, where all the crucified join in a chorus of "Always Look on the Bright Side of Life." Unlike the humorless depiction of the crucifixion in Mel Gibson's *The Passion of the Christ*, the always-sincere and ever-faithful Monty Python troupe was somehow able to intuit just how outlandish this scene in Mark really is. It's truly a revealing insight, for it suggests that it is only through an absurdist

deconstruction of the sort Monty Python provides that anyone can even begin to grapple with the a/theistic fissure that
the cross represents.

Finding New Conversation Partners

If Bowie's numerous collaborations and constant explorations
of musical forms that were unfamiliar to him are any indication, no one gets very far in answering these what-if questions unless they are able to find new conversation partners.
This is especially the case when darkness descends, as it does
on Golgotha in the middle of the day (v. 33). For when darkness has not simply consumed the landscape but has come
to constitute the very conditions of existence, those who
have only ever known a world of light will be of little help.
Thus, Bowie, Cohen, and Cave are ideal conversation partners because they know the darkness, and they know it well.
They are able guides, well equipped to lead fellow travelers
not out of the darkness, but deeper—much deeper—into it.

Nick Cave's musical-aesthetic reflections on his own personal tragedies are particularly illuminating in this regard.
Some traumas, like the death of a child, change people in
irrevocable ways. Recall that, for Cave and his wife, their
ability to go on living in the wake of such tragic loss had
nothing do with finding answers to the question of why.
Rather than engage analytically with the catastrophe that
descended upon them, they posed the creative question of
what if. Their answer was to be happy—not as a way of

ignoring the tragedy or pretending it somehow makes sense, but as an act of revenge.

It's a risky move, in part because it requires the victims of suffering to stare directly into the heart of darkness, but also because it creates the potential for further loss and heartache. In this way, Cave is like a modern-day Job, a man who lost every single one of his children on the same day (Job 1:18–19), only to find himself at the end of his life with children once again (Job 42:13). Many understand the final act of Job's life as a kind of restoration or vindication, as the enactment of justice for a wholly innocent man. But anyone who has ever lost a child knows that no number of future offspring could ever replace the child who died. To suggest otherwise is an obscenity, but this is exactly the way in which the story of Job is often accepted and understood.

Interestingly enough, Job himself moves in quite a different direction, and it's one that finds a great deal of resonance with Nick Cave's approach to the trauma of losing a child. Of all the information the text provides concerning Job's supposed restoration, it details that, along with his sons, he gives an inheritance to his three daughters, whom he names Jemimah, Keziah, and Keren-happuch (Job 42:13–15). Literally translated, these names mean "dove," "cinnamon," and "eye shadow," which just so happen to be the names for women's cosmetic embellishments in the ancient world. In other words, after enduring unimaginable tragedy, Job names his daughters using aesthetic categories. Although one can only speculate, it could be that, like Nick Cave, Job decided to be happy and to celebrate his daughters' beauty not as a way of ignoring his prior loss, but as an act of revenge. And the only means he had for enacting this kind of revenge was in and through humanity's greatest creative act—the generation and naming of life.

All this to say, in order to ask "what if?" of the crucifixion, new conversation partners are needed, whether they be biblical (Job), musical (David Bowie), or comical (Monty Python). Otherwise, it becomes very difficult to make any sense of the cross and the all-consuming darkness it entails. Lest anyone forget, in the Christian tradition, the period of time captured in the fifteenth chapter of Mark's narrative also goes by the name Good Friday. But it makes precious little sense to consider any of what transpires in this passage to be good. In all fairness, the community of faith calls this day Good Friday only in retrospect—that is, in light of Jesus's Easter resurrection. But as the story of Job and the music of Nick Cave reiterate, the death of a child can never be considered good, regardless of the kind or quantity of blessings that might come at a later time. In Jesus's crucifixion, a child surely dies, and a father most certainly loses a son.

The noontime darkness in Mark's Gospel signals a moment of genuine godforsakenness. It is a moment in which the world experiences firsthand the death of god as the sonlessness of the father and the fatherless-ness of the son. This is good not in any moral sense, but in the sense that this kind of godforsakenness presumes a thoroughgoing nihilism—one that construes the death of god as a new beginning rather than a despairing end. As it turns out, the author of Mark was a nihilist long before Nietzsche. However, given the human propensity to turn away from darkness or pretend as if it were something other than what it truly is, Nietzsche helps crack open the kernel of a/theism that always already resides in the dark heart of the crucifixion story. Indeed, just as the madman in Nietzsche's *The Gay Science* says, "'Where is God gone? . . . We have killed him,—you and I! We are all his murderers! . . . God is dead! God remains dead! And we have killed him! How shall we console our selves, the most murderous of all murderers?'"[3]

Nietzsche's madman was not addressing religious people. He was addressing his post-Enlightenment contemporaries—those who had effectively done away with God but continued to prop up their refined moral sensibilities with the very same God they claimed no longer to need. Nietzsche was thus attempting to get his audience to come to terms with the same reality as the author of Mark: God really has died. We (i.e., all of us) really did kill him. And we desperately need to acknowledge that, as a result, the world is no longer the same. The death of god has fundamentally and irrevocably shifted the (moral, religious, political) coordinates of our lives.

If the death of god actually does constitute a new beginning, and the darkness of Golgotha is now a starting point rather than an end, then Nietzsche, Cave, Bowie, Cohen, and the Gospel of Mark all help address the question of how anyone could possibly move forward, given all that has transpired. This eclectic and somewhat unexpected set of conversation partners joins together in an attempt to go on living in a permanently post-traumatic state.

Juxtaposition

Leonard Cohen stands out among the rest of this group in that he frequently uses biblical material in his music to rail against the divine, which is why he is sometimes mistaken as a sincere believer. However, Cohen employs religious language not as a way of proclaiming his belief in God, but as a means of addressing his deep and abiding ambivalence toward God in the face of life's complexities. In this regard, he's in good company. Jesus, while dying on the cross, does the very same thing: he uses the word of God to accuse God of divine abandonment (v. 34).

It is not insignificant that Mark places the words of Psalm 22 in the mouth of the dying Jesus: "My God, my God, why have you forsaken me?" (v. 34). Originally attributed to David, these lines are taken directly from Israel's liturgical canon—poetic utterances deployed in the context of corporate worship. Psalm 22 is known as a psalm of complaint, and as the poem unfolds in its entirety, it becomes clear that the psalmist is directing this particular grievance toward a God who actively listens and faithfully responds to the people of Israel:

> You loyal followers of the Lord, praise him!
>> All you descendants of Jacob, honor him!
>> All you descendants of Israel, stand in awe of him!

For he did not despise or detest
    the suffering of the oppressed;
he did not ignore him;
    when he cried out to him, he responded.
(Ps 22:23–24 NET)

Interestingly, these latter verses of the psalm never cross Jesus's lips. Given the way crucifixion works, it may be that he suffocated before he could recite every line. But it is far more likely that, in spite of what the second half of Psalm 22 claims, when Jesus cried out to God, there was no response. There was only silence. By forsaking Jesus, God joins with the Roman soldiers, the religious leaders, the curious passersby, and even the criminals hanging on the surrounding crosses and commits apostasy. Worse yet, it is divine apostasy. In response, Jesus calls this God to account, using the very words the nation of Israel had used for centuries to praise and honor their beloved God. In so doing, Jesus turns God's own sacred text against God's self—a second apostasy. The Son forsakes God.

The profound incongruity of Jesus serving as the embodiment of godforsakenness constitutes what Paul would later call the scandal of the crucified Christ (1 Cor 1:23). As Paul suggests, it's a logical stumbling block to suggest that, in the crucifixion of Jesus, God somehow died, for everyone knows that gods don't die. It doesn't make any sense. But it verges on the absolutely absurd (Paul calls it foolishness) to go one step further and suggest that God is an a/theist, or that Jesus's cry of godforsakenness on the cross somehow articulates the core of the Christian gospel, otherwise known as the good news. That's like calling an electric chair a "mercy seat."[4]

The juxtaposition of seemingly incompatible ideas (e.g., the son of God as godforsaken or an instrument of death as an instrument of mercy) is often too counterintuitive, radical, and challenging for staid sensibilities. It's partly why people, especially religiously oriented people, almost always misunderstand what Jesus is saying. Despite the fact that he is quoting well-known Scripture with his final words of apostasy, it seems that none of the spectators have any idea what he is talking about: "He must be calling for Elijah. Yes, let's see if Elijah comes to rescue him!" (vv. 35–36). It may also be why, for everyone who was not a firsthand witness to these events, one of the most prominent responses to the death of god was, is, and continues to be art, music, image, and narrative. Indeed, there has been no shortage of artwork focused on the crucifixion, whether historically speaking or in the current, post-theistic context, likely because there is no better mode through which humans might capture, express, and otherwise explore such a profound incongruity than in and through aesthetic means.

All told, then, the divine apostasy occasioned by the cross exposes the limits of human modes of knowing that traffic exclusively in syllogistic reasoning or deductive logic. Approaching Jesus's cry on the cross in these ways is like attempting to determine how much a compelling piece of music weighs. It's a category mistake. Along similar lines, to suggest that, in the crucifixion, God became an a/theist is not to accuse the Father or Son of blasphemy, nor is it to dabble in illogical untruths that lead to some other kind of heresy. It is rather to reject the logic of the atheism/theism polarity altogether, acknowledging instead that a distinctly a/theistic aesthetic—a mood or sensibility toward life that seeks new coordinates in the wake of the death of god—resides within the heart of the Christian faith. In fact, taken from this perspective, what is truly heretical is any attempt to make sense of, rationalize, or otherwise logically explain Jesus's despairing cry to the God who had so obviously forsaken him.

Living with Contingencies

According to the Markan narrative, with his dying breath Jesus "cried out with a loud voice" (v. 37). Unlike the earlier recitation of Psalm 22, the text doesn't state what, if anything, Jesus actually said at this point. It could simply have been an inarticulate groan—precisely what would be expected from someone dying under these conditions. But it also could be that the author who crafted Mark's account of the crucifixion had something else in mind. Like the well-worn line from Leonard Cohen's "Hallelujah," this detail about Jesus crying out with a loud voice functions as a way for the central figure in the story to say "maybe." Maybe there's a God above. But of course, maybe there isn't. As his life slips away, Jesus equivocates. He stutters. He is uncertain. It's an uncertainty that needs to be voiced, but it's something too deep for words, so all he can manage is a guttural scream.

The tearing of the temple curtain further reinforces this

sense of contingency and uncertainty (v. 38). The curtain separated the outer sections of the temple from the holy of holies, which was thought to be where the Shekinah—the very presence of Yahweh—dwelled. No one other than the high priest was allowed to enter this space, and even then, only at certain times of the year. The author of Hebrews invokes the tearing of the veil as symbolic of Jesus's high-priestly role, suggesting that, in Jesus's death, the barrier that once stood between God and humans is no more (Heb 10:19–21). But given that Mark's narrative includes only two portents (the noontime darkness and the tearing of the veil), a less absolute interpretation of Mark's account is in order. It may very well be that the same divine absence experienced by Jesus as literal darkness carries over to the place where God was once thought to be present. If this were so, the tearing of the veil would not be a symbol of humanity's new-found access to God's presence, but rather, a narrative device designed to underscore the presence of God's absence. As a narrative bookend to the midday darkness, the temple curtain is torn in two, and perhaps for the first time, everyone sees that there is nothing behind the veil. Maybe there never was.[5]

Contingency goes all the way down, which means that chasing absolutes is a fool's errand. The challenge, then, is learning how to live with contingencies and uncertainty—how to live with the ever-present maybe that is always on the tip of one's tongue. It's by no means an easy or comfortable position in which to exist, but as Voltaire once said, "Doubt is not a pleasant condition. But certainty is an absurd one."[6]

Avoiding the Theological

Upon Jesus's death, the Roman centurion standing at the foot of the cross voices his interpretation of all that has taken place: "Truly this man was God's Son!" (v. 39). Significantly, he is the only character in this scene who offers up any sort of theological reflection or *theo–logos* (quite literally, words about God). No one else utters a single word. Instead, a godless Roman centurion is the only one who articulates any sort of faith. It matters a great deal that, as the "faithful" followers of Jesus remain silent (v. 40), this centurion articulates something along the lines of what Simon Critchley calls the "faith of the faithless." Indeed, for Critchley, just as it is with the story of the centurion in Matthew 8, so it is with the centurion in Mark's narrative. That is, the one who is not a follower of Jesus is the only person in the story capable of displaying the kind of faith that has the potential to enact life.[7]

All this to say, there is theological warrant for avoiding the theological. Christians would therefore do well to consider placing an extended moratorium on all things *theo-logos*—to just shut up for a while and allow those who have "no" faith to speak. Doing so would certainly create space for the a/theistic faith of a Roman centurion (or a David Bowie, or a Nick Cave, or a Leonard Cohen), but it would also shed a unique light on that which Christ himself embodied and enacted—namely, the death of god on a Roman cross.

Of course, to entertain these thoughts with any kind of seriousness is, in some ways, to challenge the very core of what it means to be a person of faith in the present moment. Nevertheless, inspired by the "faithful" followers of Jesus who said nothing while the "faithless" centurion identified Jesus as the Son of God for all the world to hear, it might very well be that, as people continue to process how to live in the wake of the death of the death of god, the most faithful thing religious individuals and communities can do is to cease doing theology altogether and let others have a turn. Who knows, in the process, they might even hear someone proclaiming the gospel. And that could be just enough to save them.

Notes

1. We discuss skulls as *memento mori* in more detail in Part III, with reference to Damien Hirst's art.

2. Eli Wiesel, *Night*, trans. Stella Rodway (New York: Bantam, 1982), 62.

3. Friedrich Nietzsche, *The Gay Science (the Joyful Wisdom)*, trans. Thomas Common (Neeland Media, 2009), 79.

4. By way of reminder, "Mercy Seat" is the title of Nick Cave's song about a man about to be executed by electric chair.

5. We owe this insight to Pete Rollins, who suggests that the Christian faith is structurally similar to a magician's act. Peter Rollins, *The Divine Magician: The Disappearance of Religion and the Discovery of Faith* (New York: Howard, 2015).

6. Letter to Frederick William, Prince of Prussia, November 28, 1770, in *Voltaire in His Letters*, ed. S. G. Tallentyre (New York: G. P. Putnam's Sons, 1919), 232.

7. "Such a proclamation is as true for the non–Christian as for the

Christian. Indeed, it is more true for the non-Christian, because their faith is not supported by the supposed guarantee of baptism, creedal dogma, regular church attendance, or some notion that virtue will be rewarded with happiness if not here on earth, then in the afterlife. Thus, paradoxically, non-Christian faith reveals the true nature of faith that Christ sought to proclaim. Even—and indeed especially—those who are denominationally faithless can have an experience of faith." Simon Critchley, *The Faith of the Faithless: Experiments in Political Theology* (New York: Verso, 2012), 249.

PART III

The How

7

An Artist: Damien Hirst

If the music of Bowie, Cave, and Cohen is any indication, then contemporary life no longer has any transcendent referent. Nevertheless, the desire for some trace of "otherness," some sense of that which goes beyond human understanding, seems to remain. As a consequence, while the entire symbolic order of modern society has collapsed in the wake of the death of god, art and aesthetic experience remain inescapable. And the same can be said of religion, even in a world from which God long since absconded. Indeed, from a historical perspective, to enter the world of art is to enter a world deeply shaped and influenced by religion. One might argue that art has replaced religion, or at least has become an environment in which sacred urges can be experienced even while religious ritual and spiritual expression are viewed with suspicion. Leonardo da Vinci's *Last Supper*, Michelangelo's *David*, Rembrandt's *The Return of the Prodigal Son*—the list goes on and on. The patronage of the Christian church through the centuries and of the great families of medieval and renaissance Europe who commissioned artists to express their pious affirmations and aspirations ensured that the foundation of art in the West had a decidedly religious flavor.

The Reformation, that great schism in Christendom that began in the sixteenth century, heralded changes for everything, including the role of art in society. Religion's influence remained profound even as the role of institutional religion in Western civilization changed. The emergence and expansion of various forms of Protestantism gave rise to a new religious aesthetic. Faith increasingly became a matter of personal and private choice, which prompted a different kind of artistic representation. Stripped of ornate statuaries and other forms of art seen as characteristic of the Catholic faith, Protestant churches destroyed religious icons, did away with prayers to the saints, and ultimately turned their aesthetic attention to the whole of the created order, leading to revolutionary changes in the scope and range of artistic expression. This religious and aesthetic protest was accompanied by a rise in the merchant class, who, armed with new riches, employed artists to capture their newfound fortune. The upsurge of family portraiture, landscape, still life, and daily-life paintings all signaled a shift in the role of art in society and the gradual disappearance of religion as a central focus of artistic expression.

As art became increasingly liberated from religious constraints and began to explore other aspects of life, overt religious themes began to fade slowly from the canvas. Of course, artists continued to explore biblical and spiritual themes in their works. After all, the Judeo-Christian tradition is one of the central pillars of Western society, and even though it now exists perhaps only in ghostly, haunting forms in major portions of Western civilization, the ideas and ideals of this tradition gave birth to the world into which we have been thrown and continue to live.[1]

Still, among both religious practitioners and those within the arts community, there seems to be a general sense that the relationship between art and religion is primarily one of animosity. Consider the uproar over Andres Serrano's *Piss Christ*, a photograph of a cheap plastic crucifix immersed in human urine, which was attacked by outraged members of certain religious groups, or the protests against Maurizio Cattelan's 2002 work *The Ninth Hour*, which featured a life-size sculpture of Pope John Paul II in full religious garb, felled by a meteorite. These are just two of the notable controversial works of art that seem to attack the beloved institutions many believe to be sacrosanct and unassailable.

With prominent examples like these in mind, one might conclude that art and religion now relate to one another according to a rather simple equation: art attacks religion, and religion protests against art. In an age of polarized sloganeering, creating easy antagonisms of this sort is quite commonplace. As a result, when it comes to exploring life and all its implications, art and religion seem to be located in two opposing corners.

However, viewing religion and art as polarities is a narrow

and decidedly naïve view of the situation. Rather than a simple opposition, the relationship between art and religion is complex and multilayered. Art and religion are both expressive meaning-making systems, each of which has the ability to create powerful and provocative statements about the world. Far from being opposites, the two overlap to a great degree in that both seek to address the human condition, inviting participants to look at themselves, one another, and the world about them with a deeper level of reflection and self-awareness.

To be sure, religion has lost much of its historic vitality and power, at least in many of its institutional forms. These are difficult days for traditional religions. But the twenty-first century has also seen the return and rise of religion in both old and new ways. Whether it be through the rise of neo-fundamentalist movements within the world's major religious traditions, or the emergence of new forms of spiritual expression and practice, the cultural and political landscape of the world continues to be reshaped by religion in ways many thought defunct.

As the twentieth century closed and a new millennium dawned, religion somewhat unexpectedly broke free from its private constraints and began to exert an influence on public life. The dominant views that characterized much of the late-nineteenth- and twentieth-century cultural landscape gave way to a resacralization, which brought new permutations of the relationship between sacred and secular, the holy and the profane. Religious impulses remain, and the core issues religion seeks to address—such as meaning, purpose, and questions of ultimacy—are still in play, but they are now explored in a wide variety of ways that often look nothing like traditional religion. It is not for nothing that art is often at the forefront of these explorations, leading the way toward a resacralization of both the private and the public.

The relationship between art and religion is and always will be complex. While both seek to express, explore, and even construct life as meaningful, art's approach is frequently symbolic and veiled, inviting multiple interpretations. Some view Serrano's *Piss Christ* as a blasphemous defilement of Christ's purity, while others see it as a contemporary icon that captures the devotion of a Catholic-born artist who seeks to understand and portray the humanity and degradation that Christ endured in his mission. In this way, Serrano's work is more complex than it appears at first blush. It generates a wide range of responses even as it seeks to prompt the viewer in a particular way. Art rarely comes with a descriptive label containing an artist's declaration of personal belief. Rather, it invites the beholder to enter into relationship with it—to understand and interpret it. In so doing, art shocks and challenges conventional wisdom, but much like religion, art also asks questions about what it means to be human, what it means to be in relation to others, to nature, and to the transcendent, in all the diverse ways that "transcendence" is understood these days.

Art can challenge, negate, affirm, support, redescribe, redefine, and offer new perspectives on religion. And like the a/theistic continuum along which they fall, religious responses to art are equally varied and wide-ranging. There simply is no singular way in which art and religion relate to one another.

To complicate matters further, "religion" means a lot of different things to a lot of different people. Simply type "What is religion?" into a search engine, and it will yield over thirty-four million responses. While an admittedly unscientific result of this kind doesn't represent the actual number of answers to the question, it does demonstrate the complexity of the question itself. It's a query that has been the subject of interest not only to theologians, anthropologists, sociologists, and cultural theorists, but also for those who seek to understand and to make sense of life in the twenty-first century. Historically speaking, religion has primarily been understood as a belief in some kind of supernatural power, which is performed through a series of rituals and other devotional practices. However, perspectives on what religion is have changed as options for relating to the divine (including the option to not relate to the divine at all) have shifted quite dramatically over time.

Thus, it is far more helpful to define contemporary religion in broad rather than narrow terms, not primarily as a particular belief system, but rather as a cultural artifact, which may or may not be associated with traditional religious faith, belief, and practices. Contemporary religion is thus embodied in material culture, which seeks to acknowledge, understand, and express notions of what it means to be human in ways that can affirm, negate, or leave open the possibility of something more—something other.

All this to say, within a context in which the referential order has indeed broken down, a seemingly incessant drive continues to prompt explorations of the something more that underscores human life, an impulse most often embodied and expressed in and through art and aesthetic experiences. By no means is the life and work of Damien Hirst the only example of this phenomenon, but his artistic productions are particularly compelling, because they provide contemporary culture with a new kind of a/theistic symbolism. As a result, they demonstrate how to resacralize a world in which the sacred has long since evaporated.

In his book *The Soul of Doubt*, Dominic Erdozain identifies a similar kind of symbolic gesture to Hirst's when he describes the spiritualist critique and rejection of Luther's dogmatic commitment to *sola scriptura* (by Scripture alone) and *sola fide* (by faith alone). Luther accuses the spiritualists of crying "Geist, Geist, Geist [Spirit, Spirit, Spirit], and then [kicking] away the very bridge by which the Holy Spirit can come . . . namely, the outward ordinances of God like the bodily sign of baptism and the preached Word of God."[2] Erdozain understands the spiritualists differently and argues that they were not so much focused on the symbolism itself but rather on the abuse of those symbols. What they wanted to reject was a "set of profaned symbols," not necessarily to reject all the "ordinances of God."[3] While Hirst rejects the whole notion of religion, he does not kick away religious symbolism. Instead he intentionally deploys religious symbols precisely because they have already been profaned, profaned by the very practitioners themselves. This move by Hirst resacralizes these symbols, but it is a sacralization of an entirely different register. Hirst does not return the symbols to their original role and function, but utilizes them to offer an a/theistic aesthetic that both critiques the profaning of these symbols and provides a new symbolic resource for navigating contemporary life.

The Aesthetic A/theism of Damien Hirst

> It's amazing what you can do with an E in A-level art, twisted imagination, and a chainsaw.
>
> —Damien Hirst[4]

A fixture on the global art scene since the early 1990s, the British-born Damien Hirst has become a widely known and controversial contemporary artist. For instance, his rotting animal carcasses floating in formaldehyde created uproar and consternation both within and outside of the art world. His life and work embodies the complex but fecund relationship between art, religion, and society. At the risk of overstatement, Hirst is one of the patron saints of the aesthetics of a/theism, in large part because his works sit firmly at the far end of the atheist position on a theism/atheism continuum.

Hirst calls himself a painter, but while he has produced many painted works, he is known primarily as a conceptual artist. Conceptualism is an approach to art in which concepts and ideas in the work take precedence over traditional methods and practices, such as painting or sculpture. The movement began early in the twentieth century largely through the work of Marcel Duchamp, who pioneered the use of everyday objects as a means of expressing artistic notions. His piece *Fountain*, which was a urinal signed by the artist with a pseudonym, is widely recognized as the beginning of conceptual art as a fixture within the artistic community. By the 1960s, conceptualism was more widely embraced by growing numbers of artists as a viable mode of self-expression. It was a means of reacting against the commodification and perceived oppressive nature of the art world and the dominance of particular art forms to the exclusion of other means of expression. Because the prevailing approach to (Western) art was seen as upholding old ideological structures that limited who and what could enter the world of art, conceptual artists sought to undermine the constraints of these symbolic structures. Urinals became sculptures, and everyday objects were installed in museums and galleries. These subversive gestures of course raised questions about the very nature of art itself, which is one of conceptualism's primary goals.

Is it art? That's a very modern question—one that traces its roots back to the explosion of options that emerged as art was freed from its prior ideological constraints. In the late nineteenth century, new technologies such as photography liberated artistic expression from its obligation to represent reality as it is actually seen. All the movements that developed in the years since (e.g., impressionism, abstraction, cubism) contributed to this most contemporary of questions, but conceptualism presses the question most of all.

In addition to stretching the limits of art's representational capacities, another important component of conceptualism is the process itself. Because the artist's idea for the piece is more important than the finished product, conception trumps execution. In other words, it's not so much about the artistic quality, skill, or integrity that a piece of art demonstrates. Rather, it's about the richness of the artist's own conceptualization as it is embodied in a given object. It's also about the ways in which viewers accept and understand these concepts. A work of art is completed by the viewer, claimed Duchamp, implying that the viewer's interpretation of the meaning of the work contributes substantively to the work itself.[5] In other words, to describe a piece of conceptual art is, at the very same time, to interpret it, and vice versa. If a work is to be interpretable at all, viewers must first digest it and allow it to wash over them.

For all these reasons, conceptual art remains a contested field among critics and viewers. Nonetheless, it has managed to create a unique space for itself in the art world. With the emergence of digital technologies, it has become one of the most compelling expressions of contemporary art, which makes it all the more significant that Damien Hirst has been at the forefront of the movement since the 1990s, when his first works were shown. Since then, he has gone on to become one of the world's most infamous artists, not to mention one of the wealthiest. He remains controversial, still manages to shock, and continues to create works that capture the imagination of many who find his art deeply meaningful and exciting. Perhaps even more importantly, however, as his ever-expanding oeuvre of both sculptures and paintings reveals, Hirst is not simply producing resonant works of art. He is constructing an entirely new symbolism for a post-secular reality—an a/theistic aesthetic. Part of Hirst's observation of religion is that it is concerned with what he calls "filling holes in people"; that is, its function is to address an existential lack. He acknowledges that he uses art to perform a similar role—to help fill the hole that exists inside everyone. "It's a way of looking at the world optimistically rather than just as a brutal swamp."[6] So his art has a function beyond entertainment or shock; it exists to address the very things that he views religion as having failed to achieve.

The Sculptures

> I was taught to confront things you can't avoid. Death is one of those things. To live in a society where you're trying not to look at it is stupid because looking at death throws us back into life with more vigor and energy. The fact that flowers don't last forever makes them beautiful.
>
> —Damien Hirst[7]

The core subject matter of Hirst's sculptures is death, and he returns consistently to this theme time and again. More exactly, his sculptures explore death from two distinct but interrelated angles. First, they invite questions about the meaning of death for the living. Second, they press viewers to consider how they might orient themselves toward death, now that traditional religion is outmoded.

Hirst addresses these questions in provocative and often shocking ways, whether by situating rotting animal carcasses in glass cases or by creating stained-glass windows using the wings of butterflies raised especially for his artistic process. His work is often viewed as cold, clinical, and lacking emotion, but the actual subject matter he explores is profoundly emotional. There is perhaps no conceptual focus more metaphysical than to ask what happens in death and whether there is life after death, both of which are central concerns in Hirst's artistic works. These are questions the great religious traditions have sought to answer for millennia, and in Hirst's work, viewers discover an avowed-atheist artist whose primary subject matter is humanity's greatest and perhaps most enduring concern: the certainty of death. In other words, Hirst wants to confront the anxiety and concerns that modern people have about death, only without the support of religion.

Medicine Cabinets, 1989

Hirst has produced hundreds of pieces of art since his public career began, but his thesis project for Goldsmith College, which consists of four early developmental works from his initial foray into gallery exhibitions, speaks to death in uniquely compelling ways. Hirst's fascination with death functions as a counter to forms of Christianity that seek to minimize death by focusing on life beyond death, presenting death as a sort of transitional state that leads to a better life, a better place, and an (infinitely) better existence. However, a central part of the a/theistic aesthetic is a focus on finitude, contingency, and the limited nature of human existence. For instance, Hirst presented his graduation project in London in 1989. Entitled *Medicine Cabinets*, the work comprised twelve identical glass-fronted medicine cabinets, each filled with various kinds of pills, tablets, and bottles of medicine. Each of the twelve cabinets bore a name drawn from the Sex Pistols' 1977 album, *Never Mind the Bollocks*. The names of the cabinets had no direct relation to the contents held behind the glass, but they demonstrated the self-referential ways in which the broader culture of punk music informs Hirst's artistic sensibility.

Never Mind the Bollocks was released at a time of great social upheaval. Britain in the 1970s was reeling from union strikes, electricity rationing, heavy taxes, major political upheaval, and increasing social angst. Punk was the musical reaction to the unrest of the times. It not only challenged societal constraints, but also sought to unleash and express the frustration and the fury many disaffected youth felt at the time. It was also a response to the commodification of the music industry. Punk was rock music's first moral-cleansing movement, resisting the commercialized and sanitized music that record companies marketed. Punk musicians sought to make noise, not music. Punk fans soaked up all the noise, reveling in the chaos and rejecting all who proclaimed order when there was none.

With titles explicitly referencing punk's seminal album, Hirst situates his medicine cabinets as a metaphor for the perceived orderliness of society. Standing in stark contrast to the sense of uniformity and orderliness evoked by their perfectly organized shelves of bottles, boxes, and bandages are the songs from the Sex Pistols album, which reject this apparent orderliness as illusory and invite viewers instead to face the chaos—to see things as they truly are. By drawing upon punk music in this way, Hirst depicts reality by contrasting it with the utopian illusion by which many choose to live.

Hirst's medicine cabinets also hint at a cultural shift—one in which the religious has been replaced by the medicinal. They present medications in an iconic form. The cabinets themselves are displayed like icon boxes, and the drugs contained within them signal the possibility of healing in which modern medicine trades. Through medicine, technology replaces theology. The miraculous becomes the possible. Death can and will be deferred. Just take these pills. Much like a Eucharistic meal, just take and eat. Drugs are thus presented as sacramental elements—a celebration of the medicinal over the theological.

Using the dynamics of the punk movement that inspired Hirst's early art forays, *The Medicine Cabinets* thus embodies the ways in which contemporary culture has turned its attention away from religion and placed its trust in medicine. The work challenges viewers to consider more fully where they have placed their trust and whether that trust might actually be misplaced. As Hirst said about this work, "I cannot understand why some people believe completely in medicine and not in art, without questioning either."[8] For Hirst, to trust medicine implicitly, without reserve, as if it really could cure every ill, heal every pain, and keep everyone alive, is to believe in something with a kind of religious zeal, even if the object of that belief is a synthetically produced psychotropic medication. It is not only to put one's faith (and fate) in a particular drug of choice, but to place one's hope in medicine's ability to deliver the user from the fear of death, if not death itself.

In this way, Hirst's medicine cabinet series constitutes a new techno-religious symbolism, one that neither acknowledges the divine nor discards the sacred. Rather, by grounding notions of the sacred in the profane, Hirst's a/theistic aesthetic imagines a reality in which the profane is resacralized, offering up a sense of the sacredness of life in its fragility and ephemerality, rather than in some sense of the ascendant or eternal. Life is neither absolutely transcendent nor wholly immanent, but sacred.

A Thousand Years, 1990, and In and Out of Love, 1991

The resacralizing tendencies of Hirst's artistic output are not limited to his medicine cabinets. For instance, Hirst unveiled his first animal installation, *A Thousand Years*, at a warehouse exhibition that he curated along with two friends. *A Thousand Years* is an installation piece, which is a term used to describe large-scale, mixed-media constructions designed for a specific space and for a temporary period. In this case, the head of a cow lies on the floor of a large glass case. Blood from the head pools on the floor. As the process of decay unfolds, maggots appear and do their work, emerging later as flies. As they begin to fly around the glass cage, they come into contact with an electronic fly killer, thus joining the cow's head in death. In a blunt, gruesome, and compelling way, the piece is a reflection on the cycle of life. As with most of Hirst's work, it presents death as a stark and brutal reality. He invites the viewer to confront the reality of life and death—that it is unavoidable and comes to us all.

If *A Thousand Years* cemented Hirst's reputation, then it was a solo exhibit the following year that marked his real emergence as the enfant terrible of the art world. Once again, he visited the theme of death, although somewhat tempered this time. Whether out of a sense that the gruesomeness of *A Thousand Years* was too much for the public or simply reflecting his more diverse range as an artist, Hirst's first solo show was less bloody. He still used animals, of course, but this time it was butterflies instead of severed cows' heads.

This shift from bloody cow's head to butterflies took place in an exhibit made up of two works: *In and Out of Love (White Paintings and Live Butterflies)* and *In and Out of Love (Butterfly Paintings and Ashtrays)*. The first work featured butterflies emerging from pupae, which were attached to canvases painted white. Flowers were planted around the room, and access to sugar water allowed the butterflies to fly, mate, and lay eggs until they died. The second piece, *In and Out of Love (Butterfly Paintings and Ashtrays)*, featured dead butterflies attached to monochrome paintings surrounding a table in the center of the room, which was covered in ashtrays full of cigarette butts and ash.

In describing these works, Hirst said that they were about "love and realism, dreams, ideals, symbols, life and death," and also "the way . . . the symbol exists apart from the real thing. Or the butterflies still being beautiful even when dead."[9] In this way, Hirst explores the theme of death by presenting the fleeting life of butterflies, whose beauty belies the fragility and brevity of their existence. It is, by extension, a meditation perhaps on the fleeting nature of human lives, played out against a backdrop of cigarette smoke and decay. Humans are born, "attached" to the earth like pupae to canvas, and then they live, fly, love, mate, fall, and die. It's the cycle of life: short, fragile, vulnerable—beautiful. Again, as with *Medicine Cabinets*, Hirst is establishing here a kind of symbolism that imagines life to be sacred not because it is ascendant and eternal but because it is fragile and fleeting. With rotting cows' heads and butterflies at various stages of life, these pieces embody and express an aesthetic vision that is responding to the collapse of the old referential order that shaped Western civilization, not through an easy solipsism, but through a resacralization of materiality.

The Physical Impossibility of Death in the Mind of Someone Living, 1991

One of his most famous pieces was shown as part of an exhibition that featured a group of artists who were termed the

YBAs, the Young British Artists. Often known simply as "The Dead Shark," *The Physical Impossibility of Death in the Mind of Someone Living* was condemned by critics but adored by the public, a rift that underscored the many ways in which the art world was out of step with the tastes of a culture moving toward the end of the twentieth century. The piece featured a tiger shark, its mouth gaping open in a threatening manner, suspended in steel-framed glass cubes. Like a modern-day triptych (a three-paneled work of art often designed for use as an altarpiece), it gave the appearance that the shark was divided into three pieces, which was actually not the case. Triptychs typically function as a sort of storytelling device, with the central panel as the primary focus; however, Hirst didn't employ the triptych in a conventional manner. Instead, much like Francis Bacon, a painter whose work influenced Hirst and who also used the triptych approach, Hirst reconstituted a traditionally religious artifact by making the panels appear to be divided when they were not and by drawing the viewer's eye forward, toward the shark's menacing jawline. What is more, Hirst filled the glass tank with formaldehyde and positioned the shark in such a way that it appeared to be living in a kind of suspended animation—even though it was dead and simply floating in embalming fluid.

Hirst said that his use of these tanks emerged from a fear about the fragility of life and a desire to create works where that vulnerability and fragility could be encased and exist. The material composition of the work is an example of this vulnerability. In spite of its immersion in formaldehyde, the shark was not fully protected from decay, so it eventually had to be replaced. And this in itself becomes part of the story. The formaldehyde is there to maintain the integrity of the shark's body—its aliveness, its ferocity. But this is ultimately impossible because everything dies. Everything decays in the end.

Once again, Hirst's work explores the unavoidable reality of death by leveraging the power of a traditionally religious (even Christian) symbolic form, the triptych, shorn of its divine referent. However, with "The Dead Shark," Hirst, like his conceptual forebears, also challenges conventional wisdom about art, especially the idea that art is something that endures. For Hirst, art is no more timeless than the religion it seeks to mimic and replace. Like the rotting corpse of a tiger shark, nothing is permanent. Nothing is eternal. Nothing escapes death. Not even art.

Away from the Flock, 1994

Much like "The Dead Shark," *Away from the Flock* also features a single animal floating in a glass container. In this case, however, it's a sheep instead of a shark. The religious connotations of the title reflect Hirst's Catholic upbringing. In Hirst's own words:

> "Away from the Flock, a flock of sheep. When a sheep gets lost from all the other sheep. Then I suppose that it has those religious connotations . . . being an outsider, not being connected to something. That was a title that came right at the very end. I don't know where that title came from. . . . Away from the Flock in a way is like: it is dead, so it is away from the living

as well in that kind of way, the flock of living things. All those things, I never really look for a meaning, it is just if it feels right, gives a lot of the right kinds of meaning. . . . And Christ is often represented as a sheep in art."[10]

Hirst's ruminations on sheep as religious symbol find echoes in the work of other artists, such as William Holman Hunt, whose painting *Strayed Sheep* (1852) also utilized the Christian notion of the sheep as a metaphor for the human relation with God.

In Hirst's articulation of this theme, however, the lone sheep floats in a glass cabinet. The glass acts as a barrier but also as a reflector. Like the painter Francis Bacon, who broke convention by placing glass over his paintings so that viewers could not help but see their own reflection staring back at them, Hirst's glass cases also invite viewers to see themselves in the artwork. As a result, engaging with his art means facing the unfaceable, looking death in the eye, with distance for now but not forever.

Hirst's animal pieces thus invite the viewer to look at death from behind the safety of a glass barrier, which acts as both a reflection of and a window into the world he wants the viewer to see. The glass case also functions like a frame around a painting, suggesting that what it contains is worthy of one's time and attention, even when it contains nothing but death. In this way, his sculptures do more than shed light on the core trauma that haunts post-secular society (i.e., the loss of meaning after the death of god). They also provide a new set of symbolic resources for reclaiming death as meaningful, not by imagining it as the gateway to another form of existence, but by calling attention to its sheer inevitability. Here, then, is the inescapable truth of Hirst's art: life matters not in spite of death, but because of it.

The Paintings

This inescapable truth also figures prominently in Hirst's paintings, which signaled a shift away from his more familiar conceptual and sculptural work. In 2005, he exhibited a series entitled *The Elusive Truth.* The exhibition was made up of photo-realistic paintings with subjects ranging from dissecting tables to football hooligans. A team of assistants under Hirst's direction created each of the paintings. The printed program for the exhibit bookends the paintings, which begin with a hospital corridor and end with a mortuary table. In between are paintings featuring football violence, suicide bombers, drugs, credit card fraud, crack addiction, and a host of other contemporary ills. Each is a simple, realistic-looking painting that invites viewers to make their own connections between the exhibit's various parts and to reflect on the implications of the work as a whole. Taken together, the artworks themselves form a new symbolism.

Hospital Corridor, 2004, Oil on Canvas

The first painting in the series is an eerily empty hospital corridor. The floors are so shiny, they are like mirrors. The all-too-familiar bland walls are covered with inconsequential mass-generated art, and the false glow of fluorescent light reflects on the floor. Somewhere at the end of a corridor like this is a delivery room, complete with a hospital bed, a team of doctors and nurses, and all the latest medical equipment to ensure the safest environment for the most vulnerable among us. In Hirst's vision, hospitals are places of transition, from sickness to health, from frailty to renewed strength, but they are also places of other transitions, from life to death. The sanitized environment captured by the painting serves as a reminder of the dangers of dirt and decay. It also evokes a sense of fragility and vulnerability. At the end of the corridor, there is a window that glows with a whiter light. Like a slightly asymmetric cross, the window's frame hints perhaps at the final transition toward a life after death.

Hirst maintains this commitment to facing mortality by bringing viewers face-to-face with their illusions—in this case, with their unquestioned trust in medicine. Humans have rejected the certainty of religion, along with its promise of immortality, and have exchanged it for the possibility of better health, or at least for longevity. Life in the modern world begins in hospital corridors just like the one depicted in this painting, and they represent the pathways each of us will eventually walk as our lives progress toward our inevitable end.

Mortuary, 2003–2004, Oil on Canvas

Once again, an empty room. This one is filled with medical equipment; a wooden stool; a scale; a stainless-steel, slightly sloping counter; stacks of white towels; large, shiny metal cabinets with closed doors; a bucket; and a broom. The walls are bare except for a large blackboard and a chart. There is no clock, suggesting that time stands till here. Actually, this may very well be where time ends. *Mortuary* stands in contrast to *Hospital Corridor* with its long, lighted path pointing toward even brighter light. Here there is no visible light source, and much of the room is cloaked in a shadow. This is a horror chamber, a mortuary, a place where the dead are autopsied and prepared for burial. The clinical nature of the environment feels much like a contemporary torture chamber. Yet none of the tools in the room—the buckets, the surgical instruments, and the table where a body will be drained of fluids, embalmed, and perhaps examined for cause of death—are meant for torture. This is simply the last stop for the human body on its path to the grave.

There is a grimness to all this sanitized organization. The scales are for weighing organs, the slope on the table is to ease the flow of water and fluid as the body is drained and washed, and the towels are to wipe up human excrement when the human is no longer able to take care of the mess. Taken along with *Hospital Corridor*, this work hints at the ways in which modern life is shaped by medicine. From the cradle to the grave, people are in the hands of medical professionals. Obstetricians welcome humans into the world, and pathologists see them out.

Framed between life and death, between *Hospital Corridor* and *Mortuary*, the rest of the paintings move through the rest of life. Six paintings focus on hospital and surgical procedures. There is also a skull painting, a close-up painting of a strand of DNA, and then a series of seven paintings of pills and medicines. These are followed by a few harrowing explorations of the devastating impact of crack cocaine on human faces. Finally, the series ends with a number of meditative paintings on vivisection, violence, and fraud. In all these works, Hirst invites viewers to reflect on life's fleeting nature and vulnerability, to consider the harshness of life and yet also to remember its fragile beauty, even in the midst of decay and despair.

In Hirst's reworking of the symbolic order, it is the medicinal rather than the religious that mediates life. Humans are shepherded through their existence via medical disciplines, practices, and tools, which can offer help and healing but can also at times turn cures into poisons (as is often the case with excessive drug use), reduce bodies to meat (as in surgical experiments), and treat creatures as mere biological systems. Hirst invites the viewer to consider that there is a beauty in human mortality that transcends even the best efforts of medicinal culture to reduce human beings to bags of flesh.

Of Hospitals and Surgical Procedures

Dissection Table with Tools, 2002–2003, Oil on Canvas

A companion piece to *Mortuary* also featured in Hirst's *The Elusive Truth* exhibition, *Dissection Table with Tools* depicts a close-up of a surgical dissection table. Again, Hirst represents the clinical nature of modern medicine in a photo-realistic manner. Traces of human flesh lie on a steel table now covered with the tools of a surgeon's work: saws, knives, clippers, scissors, discarded surgical gloves, and a sheet hinting at a body lying just underneath. All of this serves as a visually stunning reminder that medicine advances by discovery and exploration at the expense of human lives and bodies. The painting itself is mined from a sculpture of Hirst's called *Adam and Eve (Banished from the Garden)*, which sheds a unique light on this work. Modern persons, the painting seems to suggest, have eaten of the tree of knowledge of good and evil. They know perhaps what they should not, that medicine can only take them so far.

Blood Sample, Anesthesia, Incision, Autopsy with Brain, and *Autopsy with Sliced Human Brain*

Each of the other paintings in the hospitals and surgical procedures section invites the viewer to consider the terrifying aspects of interaction and engagement with the medical profession. In *Blood Sample*, Hirst captures the moment in which the needle pierces flesh. The syringe fills with almost-black fluid, an allusion perhaps to the notion that life and death are in the blood. The idea is that human beings give of their vulnerability to be diagnosed, to offer help to others, and in this simple procedure, so much of life and death occurs. Again, Hirst puts an unflinching gaze on the various dependencies created by modern medicine. He turns what have become somewhat-everyday encounters with bodily invasion into stylized moments, creating a sort of visual iconography by employing images not of saints of old but of the tools of modern salvation through medicine.

The theme of syringes continues with *Anesthesia*, although this time, the process is reversed. A gloved hand holds a tube into which a syringe needle is inserted. The plunger is almost at the bottom of the syringe tube, while a faint yellow liquid travels along the length of the needle. In this painting, nothing is drawn out, but rather something is fed in, something that suspends time and space for the patient, putting them in a limbo-ish state—passive, immobile, corpse-like, yet not dead. They are in a form of suspended animation, much like the animals in Hirst's glass cubes. Says Hirst, "I tried to make a painting that gave a feeling of going under, of helpless trust in others, a faint hope beyond the fear of death."[11]

Hirst is enamored of small instruments like these: needles, syringes, and scalpels. They are small but wield immense power over the human condition, and Hirst presents them as iconic elements. There is a calm, almost meditative quality to his medicinally focused paintings, but the overriding theme in all of them is the vulnerability and frailty of what it means to be human. Making oneself vulnerable to another, particularly to someone in charge of medical procedures, is one of the few spaces in modern life that does not require one to be self-sufficient. Placing one's life in someone else's hands requires an exceptional amount of vulnerability, yet from the perspective of Hirst's paintings, it is also a mundane occurrence, happening thousands of times every day in hospitals all over the world as people receive medical help for what ails them.

Incision explores the immense power of one instrument in particular—a scalpel. The painting depicts the hands of a surgeon, one wielding the surgical tool while hovering above a small piece of visible flesh, and the other resting on the body of the patient. The patient is anonymous to the viewer and to the surgeon, covered by a familiar blue surgical gown. The surgeon's hands, clad in white latex gloves, look robotic. Behind the hands, in the painting's background, the outline of a breathing apparatus and drug-dispensing tubes can be seen. It's as if the whole thing is a kind of factory. There is a certain robotic feel to it all, suggesting that, in hospitals (at least in this hospital), emotions must be held in check. Some manner of dispassionate distance must be observed, especially concerning matters of life and death. Of course, the paradox of the scalpel featured in *Incision* is that it is a tool capable of slicing something open to provide a pathway to healing yet, at the very same time, able to cut flesh in order to destroy it. To go under this knife, one must become ultimately vulnerable, willingly submitting to someone who wields an instrument than can destroy or restore.

The final two paintings of the medical series focus on autopsy. *Autopsy with Brain* returns to the mortuary, in particular to the scale that hangs in the corner of the empty room. This time, however, a person is in the room. In this environment, the human figures are completely covered and, as a result, appear somewhat disembodied. In this case, all that can be seen is a person wearing a surgical mask and gown, holding a human brain in their hands, about to place it on the scales in order to weigh it. *Autopsy with Brain* echoes paintings by Dutch Golden Age artists such as Vermeer, whose work, *Woman Holding a Balance* (1664) features a wealthy Dutch woman holding jewelry scales in the foreground, while a Catholic painting of the last judgment appears behind her. The painting contrasts worldly wealth with the wealth or poverty of the soul. However, in Hirst's modern rendition of the weighing of a life, viewers find themselves confronted not with the weighing of a "soul," but rather with the weighing of a brain.

Thus, once again, these paintings focus not only on the reality of death, but also on the possibility of discovering through death information that might offer clues to the functions of the body (e.g., the brain) and perhaps even the meaning of life (e.g., the soul). For instance, the sequential work *Autopsy with Sliced Brain* shows a gloved surgeon using a scalpel. This time, rather than weighing a human brain, the task is to slice it into segmented portions—to search for clues buried in this gray matter that might unravel its many mysteries. Hirst himself has said that the slices of brain remind him of the Italian food dish saltimbocca alla romana, and that dissection seems "like an odd way to unravel the mysteries of the human mind."[12] Odd indeed.

Of Skulls and DNA

Even though *Anesthesia*, *Incision*, and *Autopsy with Brain* are rather short designations for these paintings, Hirst has a habit of using quite lengthy titles for many of his works. He links the practice to a belief that, if artists are going to title their work, they might as well try to say something when they do. This is very apparent with *Homo floresiensis, a New and Diminutive Species of Human Being Has Been Discovered* (2004–2005, oil on canvas). It is a simple work featuring two human skulls of different sizes portrayed against a stark black background. In art, skulls fall into the category of *vanitas* objects, which are items like skulls, hourglasses, and old books often used to invite sober reflection on existence. They act as a reminder that life is short and uncertain. *Memento mori* ("remember that you have to die") describes the function of skulls in particular. They serve as a reminder of death, an object that encourages viewers to contemplate the brevity of existence. Every skull is unique, but as *memento mori*, they share a common theme: everyone has a skull, but among the living, skulls are never seen. Therefore, Hirst's skulls represent the side of life that often goes unseen and unsaid—that which is ever present but always just out of view.

Skulls also feature heavily in Hirst's later work. *For the Love of God* is a real human skull wrapped in platinum and encrusted with millions of dollars' worth of diamonds. It is reputedly the most expensive piece of contemporary art ever made. The skulls featured in *Homo floresiensis* are simpler and more classically rendered. They offer a meditation on scientific reductionism, another theme that Hirst hints at in his work. In spite of the triumph of modern science and the incredible achievements made in its name, the medical sciences have a tendency to practice a sort of reductionism, thereby often missing the irreducibly symbolic nature of the artifacts and materials with which any science engages. According to Hirst's aesthetic vision, the human skull is so much more than bone, the brain so much more than the sum total of its parts. Through the simple act of painting or decorating skulls, Hirst declares these artifacts to be art, which is to say that they are symbolic of the deeper reality lying just beneath the surface or, in this case, just below the epidermis.

As if to address both the symbolic depths of the human body and the reductive tendencies of modern medicine, *The Structure of Deoxyribonucleic Acid* (2003–2004, oil on canvas) is a meditation on medical humility. Hirst modeled a strip of human DNA, with each atom represented by a colored ball: white for hydrogen, black for carbon, red for oxygen, and blue for nitrogen. The piece has a playful, childlike tone, which stands in contrast to the intensity of some of the other works assembled for the exhibit. Nevertheless, the larger themes are still present. Hirst focuses the viewer's gaze on one of the core symbols of scientific progress, the DNA strand, which has been transformative for understanding the makeup of life on earth. In Hirst's hands, DNA functions as a quasi-religious icon, highlighting the ways in which modern persons have devoted themselves to the life-giving potentials of science. His work also offers up a glaring reminder of how much remains unknown and misunderstood. In so doing, Hirst reappropriates the power of a thoroughgoing materialist symbol for a/theistic purposes.

When viewed in the context of Hirst's overall artistic project, DNA becomes symbolic not of humanity's unlimited potential, but of humanity's limits. It is a call for humility, an acknowledgment that, in spite of the torrent of information about human bodies that medical science continues to reveal, conceptions of what it means to be human remain childlike, perhaps even naïve. The painting thus highlights how much faith is required in order to place one's trust—and, indeed, one's hope—in the possibilities of DNA research. In this way, this work, much like many of Hirst's paintings, offers up a new kind of symbolism, one that is born of the retranscription of traditional religious rites and rituals combined with a ritualizing of modern practices and inventions. This is a new symbolism focused on acknowledging both the beauty and brutality of life, a symbolism that is particularly well suited for navigating post-secular life.

Of Pills, Pills, and More Pills

Drugs of all kinds make up the bulk of the paintings created for *The Elusive Truth* exhibit. Returning to his graduate thesis subject, Hirst made a series called "Fact Paintings" that cover most of the elements of human relationships with drugs of every kind, legal and illegal, and offer up ample room for reflection on what it means to live in a medicated society.

With portrayals of pharmaceutical packaging for drugs such as Ativan and shelves of neatly painted single pills in *The Tears of Jesus* (2003–2005, oil on canvas), Hirst meticulously situates medicines in ways that make them look perfect and pure at first glance. Upon closer inspection, however, each comes with lists of potential side effects that are miles long. In this way, he challenges the promotion of these drugs as a panacea. He highlights the many ways in which contemporary persons have become utterly dependent upon pills of every kind to address all that ails them (whether physical or emotional), so much so that they continue to enrich big pharmaceutical companies that ensnare countless people in webs of addiction to pills that don't always deliver on their promises. And by explicitly referencing Jesus in the title of the work, the unspoken commentary is that many use religion in a similar way.

In pieces like *The Tears of Jesus*, Hirst juxtaposes religious symbolism with the symbolic power of a material artifact like drugs, which once again suggests that he is redirecting rather than rejecting the religious impulse. In this way, his work bears similarities to Sigmund Freud's *Civilization and Its Discontents*, in which the psychologist analyzes the human desire to deal with the pain of existence through what he terms palliatives.[13] According to Freud, there are three principle palliatives, one of which involves the ingestion of intoxicants. These are drugs and alcohol and other kinds of stimulants, substances that don't necessarily alleviate pain or suffering but in some way make users insensitive to it and therefore able to cope with it. Freud did not directly address modern pharmaceuticals as Hirst does, but they would seem to fall quite nicely into his categorization of a palliative. The problem with palliatives is that they can often become a cause rather than a cure. Alcohol can alleviate misery, but drinking too much alcohol runs the risk of alcoholism, which brings additional misery.

Along similar lines to Freud, Hirst addresses the religious symbolism that attaches itself to certain medications through the portrayal of two white pills that look like Communion hosts. *Two Tablets (V)$(H)* (2004–2005, oil on canvas) shows the two pills reflected in the mirrored surface of a medicine cabinet shelf. The painting's shadows double the number of pills, suggesting that these pills hold much more than may be visible. Hirst makes this connection explicit in his catalog comments on the piece: "It can't be an accident that they look like the host used in the Holy Eucharist. The body of Christ, is it that hard to swallow?" Note how Hirst inverts both the sacred and the profane at one and the same time. It is modern medicine as Holy Eucharist. But it is neither "The body of Christ, given for you" nor "Take your medicine as prescribed." Rather, it's "The body of Christ, is it that hard to swallow?" It's a rhetorical question that presses viewers to consider whether, like medicine, religion is an equally hard pill to swallow—a timely and a/theological question if ever there was one.

Of Crack Cocaine and Credit Cards

The final section of *The Elusive Truth* explores themes related to the tragedies of life in modern times. Beginning with *The Devastating Impact of Crack Cocaine* (2004–2005, oil on canvas), Hirst tackles the crack cocaine epidemic that devastated numerous communities across Western culture in the early years of the new millennium. The paintings in this small series are all portraiture, with the first featuring a strip of small portraits of a real person who died from crack cocaine. Hirst mentions elsewhere that crack cocaine is the personification of the devil on planet Earth.[14] In important respects, these paintings gave him the space to examine both the unstoppable nature of drug addiction and the government's complicity in the epidemic.

Two more paintings in the series also feature portraits, *Addicted to Crack, Abandoned by Society* (2004–2005, oil on canvas) and *The Devil on Earth* (2005, oil on canvas). Both comment on the devastating impact that illegally manufactured synthetic drugs have had upon people's lives. Magnifying the faces of individuals that are slowly devolving as a result of both legal and illegal drug use, these paintings suggest in no uncertain terms that contemporary people are trapped within cycles of addiction and abuse that seem to go on unchecked and unabated in the broader culture as well. In spite of the promises of panacea made by big pharmaceutical companies, no one, it would seem, has found this promised contentment. Indeed, even though the crack epidemic finally petered out, opioid addiction is at an all-time high in the

United States. It now represents the greatest threat to US life expectancy in recent memory.

Interestingly, a meditation on money follows this focus on drug addiction. *Credit Card Fraud* (2004, oil on canvas) shows a pair of hands wearing surgical gloves and stealing credit card information via a small piece of technology. On a table, hundreds of stolen credit cards await the theft of their digital content. Here, Hirst ventures into deeply theological territory—money—the love of which is regarded biblically as the root of all evil (1 Tim 6:10). It might seem strange to put a painting about credit card fraud in a section on violence, but in many ways, the continual pressure to participate in a consumer economy is its own kind of violence. Modern persons are constantly encouraged to extend themselves beyond their means, and banks are there to offer easy indebtedness in the form of a credit card or two. Of course, according to Hirst's vision, this kind of credit-based economy has simply exposed a different set of vulnerabilities. Hirst invites the viewer to reflect on the power that money and banks hold over the whole of modern life.

The final two paintings, *Football Violence* (2004–2005, oil on canvas) and *Suicide Bomber, Aftermath* (2004–2005, oil on canvas), both explore unnecessary violence. *Football Violence* portrays a soccer fan injured in a fight, blood running from a wound under his eye and rolling down his face. The painting has a religious feel, rather like an icon that weeps. The man in the painting has a glazed look in his eyes that makes him appear statuesque, which only adds to the iconic quality of the piece.

The second piece on violence, *Suicide Bomber, Aftermath,* is much less personal and possesses a different kind of intensity. Drawn from real-life events, it captures the aftermath of the detonation of a car bomb in Iraq, which occurred as police were trying to stop the suicide bomber's vehicle. The central focus of the painting is the hood of the bomber's car, streaked with a long line of blood. The windshield of the car is peppered with bullet holes. Taken as a whole, the painting captures the essence of the terrible impact of the Iraq war and the ongoing tragedy of a world filled with multiple forms of religious fundamentalism that use violent acts of terror to advance their causes. For Hirst, much of the violence in the twenty-first century has a particularly religious shape to it. And at the height of the Iraq war, Hirst waded into the fray by inviting the viewer to face this twenty-first-century reality in all its brutality and gore.

All told, Hirst's work is decidedly dark. He remains an artist who likes to shock viewers and confront them with otherwise grim realities. Blood, decay, death, and brutality are Hirst's primary artistic instruments. Many dismiss his macabre subject matter as a simple marketing ploy. But this kind of response does a great disservice to him and to his growing body of work. A world in which the referential order has broken down or been blown apart remains a precarious one, and this reality often goes unnoticed or overlooked, both in the art world and the world of religion.

People hoping to navigate this new terrain have little with which to orient themselves, especially when they are constantly caught up in the horror of what might still lie behind it all. Therefore, new coordinates are needed, and in more ways than one, Hirst's art provides the necessary symbolic resources for this kind of resacralizing project. In fact, Hirst's thoroughgoing commitment to exploring the inescapable truth about life (i.e., we are all marching toward death) makes his art profoundly theological. But as he creates works that symbolically explore the limits and horizons of human existence and transform religious ideas and symbols into new forms without an appeal to traditional notions of the divine, it also makes him—an avowed atheist—a theologian of sorts. Better yet, it makes him an a/theologian.

Notes

1. Mieke Bal, "Postmodern Theology as Cultural Analysis," in *The Blackwell Companion to Postmodern Theology*, ed. Graham Ward (Malden, MA: Blackwell, 2001).

2. George H. Williams, *The Radical Reformation*, 3rd ed. (Kirksville, MO: Truman State University Press, 2000), 1249. Cited in Dominic Erdozain, *The Soul of Doubt: The Religious Roots of Unbelief from Luther to Marx* (New York: Oxford University Press, 2016), 39.

3. Erdozain, *The Soul of Doubt*, 39.

4. Quoted in Philip Hensher, "Damien's Pop-Up Manifesto," *Telegraph*, September 6, 1997.

5. Marcel Duchamp, "The Creative Act," in *Salt Seller: The Writings of Marcel Duchamp (Marchand du Sel)*, ed. Michel Sanouillet and Elmer Peterson (New York: Oxford University Press, 1973), 140.

6. Sean O'Hagan interview with Damien Hirst, in *Damien Hirst: New Religion* (London: Paul Stolper/Other Criteria, 2006), 12.

7. Quoted in Elizabeth Day, "Damien Hirst: 'Art Is Childish and Childlike,'" *The Guardian*, September 25, 2010, https://tinyurl.com/y9l9topm.

8. Damien Hirst, quoted in Arthur C. Danto and James Frey, *Damien Hirst: The Complete Medicine Cabinets* (London: Other Criteria, 2011), https://tinyurl.com/y8p3j4b5.

9. Danto and Frey, *Damien Hirst.*

10. Danto and Frey, *Damien Hirst.*

11. Danto and Frey, *Damien Hirst.*

12. Danto and Frey, *Damien Hirst.*

13. Sigmund Freud, *Civilization and Its Discontents*, trans. James Strachey (New York: Norton, 2010).

14. Damien Hirst, *The Elusive Truth: New Paintings* (London: Gagosian Gallery/Other Criteria, 2005), 17.

8

Universal Triggers

If horror fiction locates contemporary life in a realm haunted by the unhuman (i.e., it identifies the where) and popular music describes the core trauma that has upended the world (i.e., it names the what), then the new symbolism generated by Hirst's a/theistic aesthetic does more than simply resacralize public and private domains. It also provides the necessary resources for navigating a world that has experienced the death of the death of god (i.e., it imagines the how).

In an important sense, Hirst's artistic productions take religion seriously enough to let it become what it needs to be in the present context. The same can rarely be said of traditional religious institutions, which are often trapped in ideas and concepts that have long passed their due dates. In this way, Hirst's work becomes an invaluable resource for modern persons precisely because it knows nothing of dogmatic certainty. Instead, his art pushes the viewer toward a kind of expansive vision that can only come about when one reflects on the singular inescapable truth of reality: death. In fact, facing death in all its raw horror is, for Hirst, the only means by which contemporary persons might be roused from their self-medicated slumber. It is the only true north that has any chance of orienting the lives of those attempting to traverse a landscape as uncertain as the present.

Art as Information

> As an artist you're looking for universal triggers. You want it both ways. You want it to have an immediate impact, and you want it to have deep meanings as well. I'm striving for both.
> —Damien Hirst[1]

Hirst creates and produces his works within the domain of conceptual art. Conceptual art is a broad field that encompasses a number of artistic practices, but the common thread uniting them all is a shared commitment to the aesthetic expression of concepts. It's about the idea or ideas behind the work. The finished product might be an assemblage of otherwise-unrelated components, or a reconfigured piece, or even a traditional painting or sculpture, but what drives the piece is the artist's concept, rather than the materials used or the objects created. Conceptual art thus stands somewhat in opposition to realist painting, which seeks to capture the world as it is seen and experienced in actuality.

Interestingly enough, conceptual art seems to be on the rise in the new century. Whether it is the hyper-photo-realism of Jeff Koons, the fragmented, fractured portraits of Adam Lupton, the performance-based work of Marina Abramović, or the conceptual sculptures of Sue Webster and Tim Noble, more and more contemporary art has its roots or at least some of its influences in conceptualism.[2]

The idea that a finished work is primarily (if not entirely) concept-driven accounts, at least in part, for the elaborate and complex titles that Hirst assigns to many of his pieces. The titles might initially seem somewhat disconnected from the subject matter, as is the case with *The Physical Impossibility of Death in the Mind of Someone Living*, otherwise known as "The Dead Shark." But for Hirst, that is exactly the point. Just imagine walking into a gallery and coming face-to-face with glass cases full of dead animals suspended in embalming fluid. An initial reaction could simply be to name the visible objects: a dead shark, or a lamb, or a cow's head. But the title, which seems to be a philosophical statement or an appropriation of religious terminology, suddenly thrusts the viewer into another frame of thought. It becomes clear that these images are not simply meant to shock (although they do), but are rather prompting a new way of thinking about existence.

Marshall McLuhan's dictum "The medium is the message" rings true here. Images increasingly drive contemporary culture; think of Instagram, Snapchat, and Facebook. According to the UK-based photo-printing service CEWE Photoworld, social-media users are uploading almost two billion photos per day onto some kind of digital platform.[3] Or to put it another way, more photos are taken every two minutes than existed in totality less than a hundred and fifty years ago.

Combine this surge in image creation with the ways in which emerging technologies encourage the use of symbolic languages (e.g., emoticons are the new symbolic language of a texting society), and it is easy to see that humans are rapidly developing an entirely new relation to images, especially as it concerns their ability to convey ideas and information.

Similarly, the images Hirst deploys are first and foremost invitations to reflect upon ideas. He is not interested in whether or not the viewers of his artwork see a shark. The shark is simply a medium through which he expresses ideas about key issues related to twenty-first-century, post-god life. In other words, he asks the viewer not to look at the images he creates, but to look through them and, by doing so, to explore the philosophical and theological questions lying just beneath their meticulously constructed facades.

The Sublime and the Ridiculous

> Whatever is fitted in any sort to excite the idea of pain, and danger, that is to say, whatever is in any sort terrible, or is conversant about terrible objects, or operates in a manner analogous to terror, is a source of the sublime.
>
> —Edmund Burke[4]

It is not uncommon to read descriptions of Hirst's work that employ words like *shocking*, *grotesque*, and *gory*. These and other negative descriptors are repeatedly used in relation to his art, but they have less to do with an evaluation of Hirst's aesthetic sensibilities and far more to do with commonly held assumptions about the function of art in the modern world and how it relates to beauty, or fails to do so.

In the first place, there is a general sense that art and art going—at least as it concerns "highbrow" or "high culture" art—is a mostly civilized and civilizing endeavor. It both demands and encourages the refinement of manners. This general sentiment is partly the result of the ways in which contemporary conceptions of art have become conditioned by visits to galleries and museums, which are often designed as a cross between a library and a sacred space. The grand design of national museums, for instance, with their Victorian sensibility, ornate facades, and long galleries filled with ornately framed paintings, calls to mind the Stations of the Cross in a Catholic church. The gallery guards monitoring the safety of the works, the hushed and dulcet tones of the docent voices, and the awed reverence with which they explain the means and motives of the artist (or creator) all create a sense that this space is hallowed ground.

Of course, the notion that museum space is hallowed ground that should be revered has changed somewhat with the emergence of modern art galleries, which tend to be stark, open, and modernist spaces where the art can be approached more informally. Nevertheless, an abiding sense of decorum often accompanies a visit to such spaces, which can be quite intimidating to some. But not all art is meant to reinforce prevailing conventions of good taste and propriety. Sometimes, as with Hirst's work, the very opposite is the case. In fact, as other societal mechanisms (e.g., religion) have fallen into disfavor, art is increasingly the medium through which modern persons engage the messiness, challenges, and traumas of human existence.

By grappling with some of the most intractable dilemmas of contemporary life, Hirst's works challenge previously held notions regarding the role and function of art. They shock, sometimes directly with their bloody gore, but at other times, such as through the butterfly series, *Doorways to the Kingdom of Heaven*, they are equal parts troubling and beautiful. In ways both traumatic and uplifting, Hirst constructs huge works of art that look like stained-glass windows made entirely of butterfly wings; however, these windows, as beautiful as they may be, are composed of corpses—butterfly corpses, no less. Needless to say, there is always a little unease when encountering works like these.

Second, it is probably safe to say that most people tend to operate with a sense that beauty should be, well, beautiful. As the Italian philosopher and semiotician Umberto Eco wrote in his masterful book *History of Beauty*, beauty is a word often used to indicate something that one likes, and the liking of something is also linked to a sense that what is beautiful is also good.[5] In other words, everyone carries with them implicit and often inarticulate ideas about what beauty is and what it isn't. And the genius of Hirst's artistry is simply that he refuses to meet anyone's expectations regarding that which is beautiful. For many people, Hirst's works are not beautiful, nor are they good. They simply do not align either with their preconceived notions concerning the role of art or with their preferences regarding the beautiful. But beauty has never been singular or static; concepts of beauty change all the time and are largely culturally determined. For instance, a brief survey of one of the primary sites where Western culture has negotiated its conception of beauty—the female form—would show how much and how often ideas about what constitutes beauty have transformed over time.

In contrast to his more immediate predecessors, Hirst has inherited a different approach to artistic representation. Pablo Picasso and Francis Bacon are among his major influences. Picasso, of course, was the master of deconstruction insofar as he created paintings and sculptures that challenged (i.e., deconstructed) the very notion of beauty. Francis Bacon, whom Hirst has named as a primary influence, was the master of grotesque imagery, known for creating strange, creature-like figures with distorted human faces. What is significant about artists in this line is that they are operating not in the realm of beauty per se, but in the realm of the sublime.

Whether discussing visual art or music or one's favorite pub, it is fairly easy to declare something "sublime" and assume everyone knows what is meant, for it is a word that has slipped into everyday vernacular as a way of describing something that is particularly cool or supremely enjoyable. But the philosophical roots of the sublime are far more specific and nuanced, and it is in this more nuanced way that Hirst's work reveals the sublime.

As a key category in philosophical aesthetics, the roots of the sublime can be traced back to the discovery in the sixteenth century of a first-century Roman work called *On the*

Sublime.[6] The unknown author is referred to as Longius. This work on aesthetics and good writing was deeply influential in the emergence of the sublime as an integral concept within culture and the arts. The sublime accrued numerous meanings but eventually came to denote that which is raised up, or set high and exalted. The concept became increasingly important in eighteenth-century Britain with the rise of landscape painting, particularly through the artistry of J. M. W. Turner, whose work marked a turn in artistic representation. His paintings of storms, shipwrecks, and alternative views of the landscape were early examples of the sublime represented in the arts.

The concept of the sublime was also central to the philosophical aesthetics of Edmund Burke, whose 1757 treatise, *A Philosophical Enquiry into the Origin of Our Ideas of the Sublime and the Beautiful*, divides the sublime into seven categories, each of which is visible in nature:

1. **Darkness**, which constrains the sense of sight (primary among the five senses).
2. **Obscurity**, which confuses judgment.
3. **Privation**, which subsumes pleasure under pain.
4. **Vastness**, which is beyond comprehension.
5. **Magnificence**, which evokes a sense of awe.
6. **Loudness**, which overwhelms us.
7. **Suddenness**, which shocks our sensibilities to the point of disablement.[7]

Together, these seven categorizations capture the heart of Burke's understanding of the sublime. For Burke, to invoke the sublime is to make reference to an encounter with something beyond common human experience—something that exceeds the limits of understanding. These categories also highlight the somewhat disorienting nature of the sublime. Darkness, privation, loudness, and suddenness are nothing if not unsettling. Thus, to view a work of art that trades in the sublime is to be disoriented or unsettled on some basic level; however, Burke understood this experience in positive terms, rather than negative.

Alongside Burke's work, the German philosopher Immanuel Kant waded into the conversation on the sublime. In *Observations on the Feeling of the Beautiful and Sublime* (1764), Kant addresses how human beings feel about enjoyment. In doing so, he draws a distinction between feelings related to the beautiful and feelings related to the sublime.[8] Feelings directed toward the beautiful are essentially pleasurable and joyful, while those oriented toward the sublime are enjoyable but accompanied by a sense of horror. Flowers, for example, might arouse feelings of the beautiful, while exposure to a raging storm would incite feelings of the sublime. Kant defines the sublime in three ways: the noble, which produces feelings of enjoyment with quiet wonder; the splendid, which produces feelings of enjoyment pervaded with beauty; and the terrifying, which produces feelings of enjoyment filled with dread or melancholy.

Burke's and Kant's work contributed to the great outpouring of sublime art in the Romantic era. The rise of the gothic novel (e.g., Mary Shelley's *Frankenstein*), with its explorations of madness and lunacy, is but one example of the ways in which terror and danger became part of the vernacular for understanding and describing the beautiful. During the Victorian era, a cultural turn toward a more sedate, refined, and less troubling form of beauty took hold of the aesthetic imagination. In 1866, Nietzsche even declared the sublime out of date. Indeed, the Industrial Revolution in many ways eclipsed the great era of sublime art and normalized a new way of being in the world. Fears about cultural shifts that once fueled interest in the beautiful and the terrible were replaced with different kinds of exploration. Yet in spite of its perceived obsolescence, the sublime did not completely disappear. As the twentieth century unfurled, the sublime made a strong reappearance in Western art. The effects of numerous wars and a host of technological innovations shifted the axis of the world once more, making space for renewed interaction with the underbelly of modern life.

As a consequence, many contemporary artists are once again drawing upon the concept of the sublime. But rather than finding the sublime in the more gothic approaches of their aesthetic forebears, contemporary artists generally locate the sublime in the complexity, challenges, and horrors of the new technological age. Today, the sublime manifests itself in the midst of a culture crippled by consumer capitalism, torn apart by religious fundamentalisms, identity politics, and political correctness, which is to say nothing of its technological, medical, and pharmaceutical dependencies. This is the aesthetic vision of the sublime within which Hirst lives and creates. It not only constitutes the cultural context that informs his artistic productions, but also shifts conversations about his works beyond the question of whether or not they are shocking to modern sensibilities. And in this way, he stands in a tradition within the art world that stretches back for centuries.

Indeed, Edmund Burke's fascination with the body, mortality, violence, pain, and power as sites that draw out "the strongest emotion which the mind is capable of feeling" captures nearly the entire scope of Hirst's work. As Hirst says, artists are "looking for universal triggers."[9] In this way, the use of a shark in his early work taps into a very modern notion of the sublime. It is a sense of beauty and elegance always already mixed with sheer terror. By leveraging this human fear of and fascination with sharks, Hirst transforms the sublime into a universal trigger. In so doing, the image of a shark suspended in formaldehyde becomes the symbolic resource by which viewers are able to think about that which lurks just beneath the surface: the inevitability not just of death in general, but of their own death and dying in a world where god is dead, too.

Conversion as Betrayal

A ce qui n'en finit pas ("To that which is never-ending")
—Michel Deguy[10]

In a world of binaries, opposites not only react but also act and interact with each other. They are dependent upon each other, neither one existing without the other. Right and wrong, beauty and truth, sacred and secular, theism and atheism—they all inform and shape each other.

In 2007, Hirst unveiled a show of his work entitled *New Religion* at the Church of All Hallows on the Wall, a church with a long and venerable history in the city of London. A large-scale installation of over fifty works, the exhibit included framed silkscreen prints, sculptures, and numerous religiously themed pieces. The show juxtaposed the beauty of religious imagery with the clinical beauty of pharmaceuticals and Hirst's ongoing fascination with the brutality of medical procedures.

Once again, Hirst contrasted the fragility of life with humanity's attempts to mitigate that vulnerability, be it through religion, surgery, or pharmaceuticals. The show's location in an ancient church added a further layer to Hirst's ongoing exploration of life and death. Hirst, raised Catholic, seems to have a fascination with the imagery and symbolism of faith even as he proclaims himself a hardcore atheist.

The interactions between religion and modern medicine were featured as an overt part of the show. A series of silkscreen prints juxtaposing medical cold remedies with Bible verses, such as John 14, Matthew 26:36–46, and Genesis 6, covered the walls. Along similar lines, the visual focal point of the exhibit was a crucifix, which was inlaid with pewter pills. It remains unclear if Hirst wants to believe in life after death, does believe in life after death, or is merely commenting on cultural obsession with immortality; nevertheless, his attempt to confront his viewers with their own mortality is as real as any religious attempt to do the same.

Hirst trades in baroque (i.e., ornate) imagery with his crucifixion piece, complete with bloody body parts arranged inside a cross-shaped box. In this fascination with religious imagery, he once again follows in the footsteps of those artists who have influenced his work. For instance, Pablo Picasso, Salvador Dali, and Andy Warhol all used religious imagery as a part of their artistic output, through the inclusion of religious symbolism and the juxtaposition of art and religion in their works. As with Hirst, it is difficult to tell whether those artists were co-opting familiar symbols, making fun of religion, or genuinely offering commentary on religion via their art. If nothing else, the ongoing appropriation of religious artifacts and symbolism demonstrates how deeply those notions are embedded in the collective cultural memory.

These artists' individual biographies reveal that, for some (e.g., Picasso and Warhol), religion seems to have played a far greater role in their personal lives than previously imagined or otherwise portrayed. Warhol, as later revealed, was in fact a lifelong practicing Catholic who, in addition to regularly going to confession, often served at soup kitchens and shelters around New York. Hirst's life and work demonstrate a similar kind of complexity, which Hirst himself has acknowledged: "I was brought up a Catholic, but I don't believe in God. I think I'm an atheist. Hardcore atheist. I'm trying to be a hardcore atheist, and then I keep making work like this."[11] Comments like these—as counterintuitive as they may seem—signal the ways in which Hirst's art might serve as a remedy for his own a/theistic turmoil and perhaps even for the viewers'.

Nevertheless, it is important to remember that Hirst is an avowed atheist or at least is trying to be. Whatever he is, he is not religious in the traditional understanding of what that word might entail. In 2009, he created a unique work for the cover of the 150th anniversary edition of Charles Darwin's *On the Origin of Species*. Entitled *Human Skull in Space*, it is an oil painting in the still-life tradition and features a ghost-like skull among other items that Hirst identifies as bearing personal significance, set against a deep-blue background that evokes the idea of floating in space. There is an X-ray-like quality to the images against this background, outlined as they are in a white-silver paint, which lends them a scientific feel. In an interview, Hirst said that he was honored to create a cover for the book, because he was moved by Darwin's keen analytical mind and his willingness to "believe in those ideas that questioned the very fabric of existence and belief in his time."[12]

This statement is a clue not only to what makes Hirst tick, but also to how to understand and engage with his work. The evolutionary theories contained in Darwin's work gave Hirst a way out of the "nonsensical creation theory" of his Catholic upbringing, which he was already questioning.[13] Hirst found his pathway out of Catholicism and into his career as an artist by rejecting Catholicism's doctrine and dogma; however, he maintains a relationship with its symbolism and some of its central themes, which are, at their core, the most human of questions. This shift away from the Catholicism of his youth was a conversion of sorts, but notably, not a de-conversion. For Hirst, it was and continues to be a constructive transition, similar to the one that many undergo in the course of rejecting an inherited tradition in favor of something more personal and meaningful. In the midst of the complexity that has come to define twenty-first-century life, where old ideas seem so weighed down with baggage that they are of little use to many trying to navigate and negotiate the digital age, these kinds of conversions are to be expected. Indeed, in certain important respects, there is no life without conversion.

In religious contexts, conversion is deemed a spiritual affair—the transition from worldliness to holiness, from darkness to light. But conversions are not limited to spiritual or religious realms alone. Conversions are passages from one state to another, and they are also in some sense a betrayal. As the French poet Michel Deguy, speaking of the apostle Paul, writes, "We are always traitors to something. . . . It was necessary for him to betray what he was, and had been, in order to be—or to 'become.'"[14]

Hirst's pieces, filled as they are with religious symbolism, effect a betrayal of sorts, but it isn't a betrayal of the profane for the sacred or holy. Rather, the conversion that takes place in and through Hirst's work opens the convert's eyes to new realities and makes the convert aware of the reversal of polarities in which it consists. This *nonspiritual* conversion, if it may be called that, is a conversion to a new worldliness, a new materialism, a rejection of a particularly religious interpretation of the world—one that much of the Western world has undergone over the past three centuries in some form or another. This type of conversion is marked by a loss of faith, which is perhaps better described as a passage from credulity to unbelief, or from belief to a/theism. Ultimately, this passage leads from a certainty and dogmatism about reality to a radical openness toward a world without divine promise that still might offer more than can be known.

Carried Away

> There is no transcendent but there is transcendence.
> —Michel Deguy[15]

Hirst's work mines the contemporary sociocultural context in which traditional faith has, for many, receded to the margins as a new aesthetic, the aesthetics of a/theism, continues to emerge in its place. There is much talk about the sacralization of art in the twenty-first century and even more about art as a substitute religion, but there might also be something else going on.[16]

While theism/atheism is a binary in which each end of the spectrum informs, reacts to, and interacts with the other, a/theism is a separate perspective standing outside the spectrum of debates that the theism/atheism continuum fosters. For too long, another binary, religious/secular, has been presented in a rather one-dimensional manner as well, describing the process of secularization as the eclipsing of the religious by the secular. The process can also be understood as part of a larger social conversion process, wherein the ways in which people have understood religious communication are being radically redefined as the sacred and profane, the holy and the unholy, the religious and the secular, are fused together.

This emerging form of sacralization creates a unique religion, or faith, wholly separate from traditional and self-referential religious communication. Indeed, just as Simon Critchley has suggested, this kind of faith is "not only shared by those who are faithless from a creedal or denominational perspective, but can be experienced by them in an exemplary manner," in large part because it is the "faithless who can best sustain the rigor of faith without requiring security, guarantee or reward."[17] A similar, although much less rigorous argument is put forth by Alain de Botton in *Religion for Atheists*, which discusses the ways in which religious ideals and practices can be appropriated by nonbelievers in order to make life more meaningful.[18] It is important, says de Botton, that they be able do so without capitulating to a belief in God or some higher power.

In a parallel move, Hirst takes religious symbols and subject matter into the region of the profane through nonreligious means of communication. In so doing, he generates a quasi-religious conversation, which in turn gives these profane environments and artworks a religious aura. This interaction is not a conversation on or about religion, but rather a blending of religious symbolism with other, nonreligious modes of communication. Whereas religious self-referential communication trades in the contrast and distinctions between immanence and transcendence, communication in these artistic spaces blurs distinctions, collapses categories, and creates new environments for reflection on timeless questions.

In traditional religion, God is viewed as transcendent (with a capital *T*), which means that God's nature and power are independent of the material world and that God inhabits a realm above all physical laws and limitations. This notion of the transcendent is usually set over and against the notion of immanence, where God is said to be fully present in the physical world and thus immediately accessible to creatures. From this view, a transcendent religious experience is a state of being in which one traverses and thus overcomes the limitations of physical existence. In fact, by some definitions, to experience the transcendent is to become independent of physical existence altogether.

Neither the absolutely transcendent nor the pervasively immanent is found in Hirst's work. He is not seeking to comment on the divine other than to affirm the death of god and the death of the role of traditional forms of religion in society. In his appropriation and use of religious symbolism, he does achieve a certain movement in his work that carries the viewer away, takes them beyond their limitations, and opens up a space for them to consider their finitude, contingency, and doubt. But this kind of boundary crossing has nothing to do with separate planes of existence populated by divine or semi-divine, superhuman beings. In this space, the space Hirst inhabits with his art, there is no such thing as the transcendent, but there is transcendence.

Put somewhat differently, to take Hirst's resacralized symbolism seriously is to cross certain boundaries and to come face-to-face with a variety of limit situations (which is why there is "transcendence" in his work). But these movements are set firmly within the "interior" of the human (which is why "the transcendent" is nowhere to be found). Hirst takes the viewer "in" rather than "up." Hirst's work thus functions like a philosophical koan, raising questions of being. Hirst can awaken questions regarding life's perplexities and challenges; however, Hirst does not seek to provide answers. Rather, his art raises the question of how to advance without answers, and how to find meaning amidst the futility, fragility, and meaninglessness of life.

All told then, the work of Damien Hirst is perhaps the chief embodiment of the aesthetics of a/theism. It functions as a revelation out of profanation that preserves the relics of religion for the worlds to come. In so doing, his art deconstructs not only religion but also the main dependencies of the contemporary world: medicine, pharmaceuticals, and consumer capitalism. Or in the artist's own words, "I want to make art, create objects that will have meaning for ever. It's a big ambition, universal truth, but somebody's gotta do it."[19]

Hirst is right. To create art that might serve as a resource for tapping into universal truth in a world that has experienced the death of god is indeed ambitious. It may even turn out to be a completely futile endeavor. Only time will tell. Nevertheless, Hirst's artistic confession explicitly names the aesthetic dimension of contemporary atheism that, even though it often goes unrecognized, is theologically significant through and through. Suffice it to say, it is virtually impossible to understand how atheism functions theologically in a post-secular world without first understanding the ways in which atheism's aesthetic sensibility is embodied in concrete artifacts like Hirst's *New Religion* exhibit and *The Physical Impossibility of Death in the Mind of Someone Living.* But the most challenging (and scandalous) theological step is the one that follows next. Namely, it is one thing to give a fair hearing to the aesthetic objects Hirst creates and the experiences they occasion. It is quite another to draw upon their symbolic language to reread the sacred texts of the Christian tradition—to do theology in and through the a/theological.

Notes

1. Quoted in "Artist Damien Hirst discusses Three Studies for Figures at the Base of a Crucifixion," Tate blog, October 18, 2018, https://tinyurl.com/y7ln9utk.

2. Where Hirst perhaps departs most from other conceptualists' major ideas is in the area of finance. Many conceptual artists resist the commodification of art and the gallery system through which it operates by creating works that are not easily bought and sold. Hirst, in contrast, has moved in the opposite direction. Rather than eschewing this commodification, he has reconfigured it by rejecting the gallery system and creating his own channels of selling and distribution for his works. He sees no problem between money and

art and has become one of the world's richest artists through his savvy and somewhat controversial financial dealings.

3. See "Photoworld – How Big Is Snapchat – Sources," public Google doc, https://tinyurl.com/y8nja6oh.

4. Edmund Burke, *On the Sublime and Beautiful* (New York: Collier, 1969).

5. Umberto Eco, *History of Beauty* (New York: Rizzoli, 2004).

6. The inclusion of a reference to Gen 1:3 in the text has led to a view of many Old and New Testament passages as examples and paradigms of sublime literature.

7. Edmund Burke, *A Philosophical Enquiry into the Origin of Our Ideas of the Sublime and the Beautiful* (Oxford: Oxford University Press, 1998).

8. Immanuel Kant, *Observations on the Feeling of the Beautiful and Sublime* (Oakland: University of California Press, 1745/2004).

9. Damien Hirst, quoted in Tate, "Artist Damien Hirst discusses Three Studies."

10. Michel Deguy, *A Man of Little Faith*, trans. Christopher Elson (Albany: State University of New York Press, 2014), 1.

11. Robert Ayers, "Interview with Damien Hirst," Blouin Art Info, May 11, 2007, https://tinyurl.com/yc7rccu7.

12. Damien Hirst, "Damien Hirst Salutes Darwin's 'Courage' in On the Origin of the Species Painting," *The Guardian*, January 26, 2009, https://tinyurl.com/y88aa24y.

13. Hirst, "Damien Hirst Salutes Darwin's 'Courage.'"

14. Many of the thoughts in this section are drawn from and inspired by Deguy, *A Man of Little Faith.*

15. Deguy, *A Man of Little Faith.*

16. For readers interested in either of these topics, Alain de Botton's work is a good place to start, especially his 2013 coauthored book with John Armstrong, *Art as Therapy* (London: Phaidon, 2016). For those interested in a theistic take on the subject, Christian Wiman's *My Bright Abyss: Meditation of a Modern Believer* (New York: Farrar, Straus & Giroux, 2013) is equally compelling.

17. Simon Critchley, *The Faith of the Faithless: Experiments in Political Theology* (London: Verso, 2012), 252.

18. Alain de Botton, *Religion for Atheists: A Non-Believer's Guide to the Uses of Religion* (New York: Pantheon, 2012).

19. Sean O'Hagan, "Damien Hirst: 'I Still Believe Art Is More Powerful than Money,'" *The Guardian*, March 10, 2012, https://tinyurl.com/y7etw7uk.

9

The Transfiguration as God's Disappearance

Six days later Jesus took with him Peter, James, and John and led them alone up a high mountain privately. And he was transfigured before them, and his clothes became radiantly white, more so than any launderer in the world could bleach them. Then Elijah appeared before them along with Moses, and they were talking with Jesus. So Peter said to Jesus, "Rabbi, it is good for us to be here. Let us make three shelters—one for you, one for Moses, and one for Elijah." (For they were afraid, and he did not know what to say.) Then a cloud overshadowed them, and a voice came from the cloud, "This is my one dear Son. Listen to him!" Suddenly when they looked around, they saw no one with them any more except Jesus. As they were coming down from the mountain, he gave them orders not to tell anyone what they had seen until after the Son of Man had risen from the dead. They kept this statement to themselves, discussing what this rising from the dead meant.

—Mark 9:2–10 NET

If there were a book in the Bible that could match Damien Hirst's fascination with death, it would surely be the Gospel of Mark. Death lives very close to the surface in the earliest account of the life of Christ. Mark's Christ cuts a lonely and sorrowful figure, surrounded by confused and mystified friends whose ignorance of his intentions often makes him angry and even more isolated. Vengeful enemies wait at every turn, and their blind allegiance to rigid understandings of religious life and practice stand in stark contrast to the one who emerges from the desert singing the song of God.

Mark's text shows a Christ-figure virtually obsessed with his own demise and driven to bleak, apocalyptic responses to his life and the world in which he lived. Indeed, as Nick Cave writes in his introduction to the Gospel of Mark for the Canongate Pocket Canon Series, the story is a "clatter of bones, so raw, nervy and lean on information that the narrative aches with the melancholy of absence."[1] As such, the story of the transfiguration can be read in terms of God's glorious presence, which is the more traditional interpretation. But with the help of artists like Nick Cave and Damien Hirst, Mark's account can also be read as a story of absence and lack.

The Clatter of Bones: Transfiguring Transfiguration

Mark's account of the life of Christ is a story of loneliness, absence, loss, and emptiness. It feels positively Nietzschean in its bleak assessment of the human condition and the fragile vulnerability of this very human Christ-figure. Needless to say, that's not always how the story is interpreted, understood, or told. Mark's Gospel is short, very short, and economic in its information. There are no genealogies or historic lineage, no birth narrative, no major discourses such as the

Sermon on the Mount. And there's no resurrection. Instead, there is a fully grown man who suddenly appears in Galilee, and through a repetitive cycle of teachings, healings, and exorcisms lays out a vision for a different way of being in the world, until he is stopped by his untimely and brutal death. He seems at odds with everything and everybody. His teachings are enigmatic and virtually indecipherable to even his most ardent followers. Miracles happen, but they seldom seem to break the status quo or grant him greater influence or fame, and his lonely life ends in betrayal, humiliation, and ultimately death. Even there, Mark's story leaves readers wanting: the information is minimal, so much so that later additions are made to "complete" the story and give it the ending it either needs or deserves, depending upon the interpretive tradition one embraces.

One of the most striking elements of Mark's account is the disappearance or absence of God. By the middle of Mark's account, God disappears from the tale in a rather dramatic way. That absence echoes in and through Christ's words as he hangs on the cross: "My God, my God, why have you forsaken me?" (Mark 15:34). These are words spoken in agony. Peter Rollins, in his book *Insurrection*, says that this cry represents Christ's experience of a "profoundly personal, painful existential atheism."[2] Christ has lost all, has been betrayed by those closest to him, and is abandoned to his fate. This a/theistic moment is not a rejection of God based on an intellectual response to arguments disproving God's existence, but rather a breakdown in response to suffering a complete existential loss that includes God. While Christ most markedly notes God's absence in his final moments on the cross, following this thread of absence in Mark's Gospel makes it clear that Jesus had actually been on his own for a while.

The beginning of God's disappearance is otherwise known as the transfiguration. It's a remarkable moment in Mark's account of Christ. The author of Mark notes that, shortly after revealing to his friends that suffering and death awaited him, Jesus goes up to a mountain to pray, taking with him three of his disciples—Peter, James, and John (Mark 9:2). While they are on the mountain, a strange event occurs. Jesus is transfigured. His clothes become "radiantly white, more so than any launderer in the world could bleach them" (v. 3). He is also visited by two figures from the Old Testament, Moses and Elijah (v. 4). Once this event ends, the disciples, who are understandably scared out of their wits, begin to come up with responses. Peter famously gives voice to their fear, and in that mad fight-or-flight energy that often accompanies terror-inducing moments, he urges Jesus to create a series of shrines and mark the moment by turning the location into a religious site (vv. 5–6). Before Christ can speak, a cloud covers them, and a voice, presumably the voice of God, proclaims, "This is my one dear Son. Listen to him" (v. 7). Silence and evaporation follow the voice, and once again, the four of them are alone on the mountain (v. 8).

Jesus commands his disciples to say nothing, and they journey back down the mountain—back to the world, back to pain, back to humanity (v. 9). In Mark's account, Jesus has now set his face toward Jerusalem and death. He leaves God behind on the mountain. When the cloud evaporates, God seems to evaporate with it and, at least in Mark's Gospel, is not heard from again. It is this very absence (i.e., the absence of God) that Christ eventually expresses from the cross (Mark 15:34), but his experience of godlessness actually begins here on the mountain.

Symbols and Metaphors

The transfiguration is often interpreted and understood in terms of brightness. It's the spectacle of the dazzling robes: "And he was transfigured before them, and his clothes became radiantly white, more so than any launderer in the world could bleach them" (v. 3). Mark uses metaphor as a way to grasp what is beyond the senses, to help the reader gain a sense of something incomprehensible. Readers, like the disciples, can recognize brightness even though they cannot fathom the supernatural vision.

There is an interesting contrast between this level of "radiant" whiteness and the kind of whiteness a launderer could achieve through bleaching clothes. According to the author of Mark, there is something otherworldly about this kind of radiance. Through a somewhat primitive but effective chemical procedure, a launderer would treat and remove a garment's stains and discolorations, and the garment would appear like new. While it remained the same garment, it was given the appearance of newness through the laundry process. Perhaps this is what Mark is trying to convey with his metaphor. In saying that Jesus's garments were radiantly white beyond the capabilities of any launderer, Mark names this whiteness as something unachievable by the most capable of humans. It's a way of saying that whatever happened on the mountain was beyond both human ability and comprehension.

The Markan transfiguration is spectacle of the highest order. Not only do Jesus's garments shine with what is generally interpreted as divine light, but two of the heroes of the Old Testament appear out of nowhere, presumably to counsel him and, at least from the reader's perspective, to affirm his divine mission and purpose. The disciples, riddled with fear, are subjected to the cloud of God's presence covering them and commanding them to listen to Jesus. It's nothing if not a moment of profound, psychosomatic, spiritual overload.

Among the more common interpretations of the transfiguration, the glory that is revealed is understood not only in relation to the risen Christ, but also in relation to the future glory that will usher in the new world. This interpretation stands to reason. After all, in Luke's and Matthew's accounts of the transfiguration, both of which add to the story, the glory of God figures prominently. The shining brightness of the clothing Jesus wears in Mark's story actually encompasses and transforms Jesus's face in Luke's version. Also in Luke, Jesus takes his disciples to the mountain in order to pray, whereas Mark simply says he "led them alone up a high mountain privately" (v. 2).

While it may be reasonable to place Mark's story into conversation with other accounts of the transfiguration, glory itself remains noticeably absent in this narrative. Mark doesn't even use the word (*doxa*), and the Gospel he tells bears little of the triumphant dynamic that is present throughout Matthew and Luke. Mark seems to labor instead on the absent presence of God. By the end of Mark's Gospel, the story has no dazzle, no brightness. In its place is the shadow of death hovering over an empty tomb. There is no triumphant resurrection story, no return of Christ after death. Christ's path in Mark is a path of loneliness and suffering that culminates in the darkness of death.

Mark's transfiguration story seems somewhat muted in large part because it has different intentions than the other New Testament accounts. For instance, metaphysics (explanatory theories about the nature of reality) takes a hit in Mark's Gospel. The idea that there are other possible worlds impinging upon this one is not entirely dismissed, but neither does it stand alone as the singular interpretation of the event of the transfiguration or the life of Christ. The brightness in Mark's story does not seem to come from within Jesus, but rather clothes him from the outside. He is draped in the divine light but not fully immersed in it. It covers him but not fully, not completely.

Interestingly, the radiant brightness of Jesus's garments is juxtaposed with the absence of light in the cloud that covers them all. The cloud has long been a symbol of God's presence and protection among the people of Israel, and is generally accompanied by a sense of light. The divine presence makes itself known through the light that emanates from the cloud. Matthew's account speaks of a bright cloud (*nephele photeine*) descending upon Jesus and his three disciples, but Mark's does not. Light is glaringly absent. There is presence in Mark's cloud, but it is the same dark presence that fills the rest of his narrative with shadows rather than light. Mark picks up this theme at the crucifixion when he writes, "When it was noon, darkness came over the whole land" (Mark 15:33). The sun, which so often signifies God's presence, is blotted out by darkness, and Jesus cries out in abandonment. In Mark's account of the transfiguration, the voice of God speaks from within the cloud, so the space upon which it rests is not completely devoid of divine presence. But the cloud also seems to hold, like much of Mark's Gospel, a mysterious darkness that is present only as the absence of light.

Given the ambiguity of the situation, it's no small wonder that Peter gets it all so wrong. He wants to build shrines, placing Jesus on the same plane as the old prophets who appeared that night. But this is not what is to happen. In fact, in this very moment, Christ is separated from the old guard, from the old story. Peter presumes that Jesus belongs among them, but he doesn't. His mission is radically different. What's striking is that the one who undergoes a transformation here is Jesus, not the disciples. They are simply witnesses—and unreliable ones at that—to an event that, in Mark's Gospel, sets Christ on a path, not to messianic glory, but to death.

As Derrida says, metaphors contain within themselves the seeds of their own destruction, which means that, rather than leading to the truth of something, metaphors actually introduce an excess of meaning that cannot be contained.[3] There are a number of ways to interpret any story, and there is always more to the story than interpretations reveal. The story of the transfiguration can be read in terms of divine presence. But Mark's account can also be read as a story of absence and lack.

In Mark's Gospel, Jesus's life reaches its consummation in tragedy. The great existential cry that falls from the lips of Jesus is both godless and profane. With darkness as his only companion, he names God's absence. This kind of death projects a certain logic across the entirety of Mark's story. It is equal parts enigmatic, complex, and existential. There is no resurrection, and there are no miraculous encounters with the risen Christ. There is only a march toward death.

In comparison with the versions in Matthew's and Luke's Gospels, Mark's transfiguration account offers a different take not only on the story's meaning, but also on sacredness itself. For Mark, presence and absence are necessary companions to spiritual life. The transfiguration is a site of Jesus's transformation and a revelation of the divine light within and around him. However, it is also a site of lack, absence, and emptiness consistent with the story that Mark is telling—one that starts with a dark cloud on a mountainside, moves to divine abandonment on Calvary, and concludes with the darkness of death and an empty tomb.

Faith at the End of Meaning

One of contemporary Christianity's core dilemmas is that it exists in a world of binaries—darkness and light, good and evil, sacred and profane, presence and absence, theism and atheism, and so on. Moreover, it tends to resist the idea that opposites can coexist. But if these binaries are rejected in favor of an organic kind of unity-in-difference, then the transfiguration in Mark's Gospel actually signals the beginning of the end for a particular understanding of God. It signals the dimming of a transcendent, metaphysical view of the divine, and the emergence of Christ as a figure connected to but no longer strictly determined by old ways of being in the world. Rejecting the pleas of those closest to him, he walks toward a death no one understands.

In this way, Mark's Gospel concerns the end of meaning. It's a journey toward death in the aftermath of God's disappearance. Religion now has a different task: how to be in a world that is meaningless. If learning how to be in a world without meaning does in fact capture the task of religion in the contemporary world, then theists in general and Christians in particular would do well to identify a new set of conversation partners who are making similar gestures. Damien Hirst, who has built a career out of shock and gore, is a leading candidate in this regard. Indeed, Hirst's stock-in-trade is death and meaninglessness explored in the sublime tradition through conceptual art. He wears his atheism on his sleeve and makes no bones about his disdain for organized religion. But as it is with so many artists who were born into the

Catholic Church, it is very difficult to discard entirely the "afterimage" or residual effects of the Catholic imagination they originally inherited.[4]

Hirst's fascination with medicine and his comparison of medicine to a contemporary religion call out blind faith in medical science's ability to heal humanity of all its physical, emotional, and psychological ills. His intimate and hyperreal paintings of surgical instruments and human brains point to the tendency among modern persons to believe that medicine will not only be able to identify every ailment, but also provide what religion never could—life everlasting. Yet as his numerous ornate skulls suggest, human life is marked by a singular, inescapable truth: the certainty of death.

Hirst continually reminds the viewer, just as he has from the beginning of his career, that death cannot be put off forever. It is the one thing that human beings cannot face and cannot overcome. Death is inevitable. Hirst's conceptual paintings and sculptures about death and its meaning and meaninglessness create a space—a theological space—in the art world, planting questions about life and death in the heart of a cultural art form. By creating contemporary *memento mori*, using works of art as objects through which to contemplate death, Hirst points both to the boundaries of life and to its locus of meaning. In this way, his work follows a trajectory similar to that of Mark's Gospel, offering a meditation on the centrality of death to life. It serves as the absent center that is always already present, planted in the very heart of reality.

In early 2017, Hirst opened a new show in Venice, Italy.

It was a gargantuan show, featuring over 190 new works, stretching over two museum spaces, and covering more than 54,000 square feet. The title of the exhibit was *Treasures from the Wreck of the Unbelievable*. The displayed works purportedly came from the wreck of a two-thousand-year-old ship that had sunk in the ocean and later had been discovered by a team of divers. Of course, this was not true; all the pieces had been created by Hirst. The pieces were in keeping with his other works: sculptures of all shapes and sizes; objects cast in marble, gold, bronze, crystal, jade, and malachite; pictures of heroes, gods, and leviathans. The show intentionally teases the viewer. It all looks like sunken treasure, but it isn't. It thus poses profound questions about truth and illusion, historical fact and myth, skepticism and faith. As Hirst said in the Netflix documentary about the creation of the show, "What makes you believe is not what's there; it's what is not there. The gap between things is where you locate your belief."[5] The truth doesn't reside in these objects, just as it doesn't reside in any object. Truth is something that emerges in the midst of an ongoing dialogue between fact and fiction, between faith and doubt, between theism and atheism.

Hirst functions as artist-priest, inviting consumers of his art to consider questions of ultimate meaning, to question reality, to explore belief, to face death, and to embrace life's fragility. As an artist, Hirst is looking for "universal triggers." This self-conscious intention suggests that, in spite of his desire for his art to have a profound and immediate impact, he also strives to create a space for something else—something more.

While he longs to be a hardcore atheist, he also seems unable to shake the very questions that faith explores. As a result, he rejects theism while allowing hints of metaphysics to emerge in his work. He trades in the profane and, at the very same time, names his works after the sacred. In more ways than one, then, his work epitomizes the aesthetics of a/theism, which is to say that it sits at the center of today's cultural dilemma, namely, determining what to do now that god has disappeared.

Notes

1. See Nick Cave, introduction to *The Gospel According to Mark* (Edinburgh: Canongate, 1998).

2. Peter Rollins, *Insurrection* (New York: Howard, 2011), 21.

3. Jacques Derrida, *On Grammatology*, trans. Gayatri Chakravorty Spivak (Baltimore: Johns Hopkins University Press, 1998).

4. For a compelling account of the Catholic "afterimage" among contemporary filmmakers, see Richard Blake, *Afterimage: The Indelible Catholic Imagination of Six American Filmmakers* (Chicago: Loyola Press, 2000).

5. *Treasures from the Wreck of the Unbelievable*, directed by Sam Hobkinson (Netflix Films, 2017).

Conclusion: A Faith of Crisis

Contemporary life is marked by numerous anxieties. Even for the most ardent believer, an unnameable and often unnoticed something is always bubbling just beneath the surface, cultivating a base-level sense of dis-ease and dis-order. The same can be said for those who claim no religious commitments. Whether one is a theist or not, a crisis of faith is always looming, always just beyond the horizon. The aesthetics of a/theism not only names the fundamental angst generated by this kind of existential threat, but also opens up possibilities for pressing deeper into and, ultimately, through the various fears and apprehensions that have come to define reality for so many.

But on another level, the aesthetics of a/theism pushes toward something a bit more radical. Functioning as both a critique of a stale and staid Christianity, on the one hand, and a site for constructive theological exploration, on the other, it advances what might be called a "faith of crisis." More than a droll turn of phrase, a faith of crisis describes a way of living

and being in the aftermath of the death of god that is neither strictly theistic nor atheistic, but a/theological through
and through. It is to suggest that the various crises of faith
brought about by contemporary culture's a/theistic sensibilities might actually be a good thing, especially if they lead
toward a more constructive engagement with the complexities of modern life.

A Crisis of Faith

> For the fate of humans and the fate of animals are the same:
> As one dies, so dies the other; both have the same breath.
> There is no advantage for humans over animals, for both are
> fleeting.
> Both go to the same place,
> both come from the dust,
> and to dust both return.
>
> —Eccl 3:19–20 NET

Theistic or not, any faith worthy of the name has gone
through some form of crisis. At least as it concerns the Christian tradition, one of the hallmarks of mature faith has long
been a deep and abiding spiritual ambivalence. From Jesus's
agonizing self-doubt in Gethsemane, to John of the Cross's
Dark Night of the Soul, to the numerous saints who followed
his teaching over the centuries (e.g., Teresa of Ávila, Thérèse
of Lisieux, and Mother Teresa of Calcutta), a pervasive, internal incongruity emerged in the life and writings of these
spiritual exemplars. Rather than eliminate or avoid their profound doubts and uncertainties, they walked through them
and with them, sometimes indefinitely.

It is also true that a crisis of faith can be vicious rather than virtuous, and in some cases, it may even result in the abandonment of faith. But it is only in a post-Cartesian world—one in which all knowledge has been reduced to certain knowledge—that the revelation of Mother Teresa's life-long experience of divine absence and spiritual emptiness in *Come Be My Light* is surprising at all.[1] The contemporary imagination is unique in many ways, but nowhere is its historical oddness more evident than in the way present-day people (especially religious people) conceive of doubt as diametrically opposed to faith or understand theism as the mutually exclusive, polar opposite of atheism. These notions persist in spite of contradictory evidence drawn not only from personal experiences of godforsakenness and divine absence, but also from the spiritual emptiness that seems to have marked the lives of those whom the Christian tradition now considers saints.

At least part of the reason contemporary persons find atheistic doubt irreconcilable with genuine faith is that, to one degree or another, everyone now operates in the shadow of Marx, Freud, Nietzsche, and the various functional accounts of religion that have followed in their wake (which focus not on the content of religious beliefs, but on the way religion functions in human society, regardless of whether the underlying beliefs are true). Indeed, if the a/theistic sensibility of contemporary art teaches us anything, it's that these three theorists were right. Religion, even (and perhaps especially) the Christian religion, often functions as a coping mechanism—a medicine or opiate that both assuages the anxiety of believers and convinces those in power that they are doing everyone a favor by maintaining the status quo.

This is Freud's primary point in *The Future of an Illusion*, in which he suggests that religious belief is most fundamentally a self-protective illusion.[2] But whether it's a contemporary narrative like *Stranger Things* or the work of artists like Damien Hirst, Leonard Cohen, Nick Cave, and David Bowie, a variety of cultural forms now posit an alternative to a strictly Freudian or Marxist account of religion. For these artists, it is only in and through their a/theistic cry of godforsakenness that they are able to capture the heart of their lived experience. In so doing, they demonstrate a genuine faith—the faith of the faithless.

In much the same way, insofar as this very same cry can be found on the lips of the faithful, it is only the faithful who are able to articulate an equally robust form of a/theism. What this implies is that, when Jesus utters *his* cry of godforsakenness on the cross, he becomes an a/theist of a different order. In important respects, Jesus is the a/theist par excellence, for it is difficult to imagine a more profound experience of divine absence than the moment when God the Father abandoned God the Son. And if Jesus provides the model that his followers are meant to emulate, then, far from a self-protective illusion, theirs is a kind of religious faith that moves toward rather than away from uncertainty and doubt.

The psychologist Richard Beck makes a similar point when he suggests that, in distinction to Freud, who conceived of all religion as a form of self-deception and existential repression,

William James (who anticipated Freud in many ways) allows for at least two types of religious experience.[3] In his *Varieties of Religious Experience*, James describes certain kinds of religion as "healthy minded," which is a category that aligns well with Freud's notion of self-delusion.[4]

But James also describes something he calls the "sick soul," which is a religious stance that actually leans into existential anxiety rather than eschewing it. The fundamental preoccupation of James's sick soul is the "existential predicament posed by our finite vulnerability in the face of death. . . . This means living with the awareness that death is an ever-present reality."[5] James calls this kind of religion "sick" not because it is pathological, but because it is grounded in existential angst. In fact, for James, it is the "healthy-minded" believer who is most susceptible to spiritual blindness and psychological self-delusion, just as Freud suggested. Yet, whereas Freud could see no reason why anyone would choose to maximize rather than minimize their anxieties through religion (or any other means), James says it's because only a sick soul has eyes that are opened "to the deepest levels of truth."[6] Thus, drawing upon James's more expansive account of religious varieties rather than Freud's more reductive account of religion as exclusively self-deceptive, Beck concludes, "In spite of the emotional price tag and cost, many religious believers appear to go in this direction—to pursue faith as a sick soul."[7]

The aesthetic dimensions of a/theism resonate with the spirit of the times, which is pervaded by a deep and abiding soul sickness. But this is nothing to be lamented, for just as

James suggests, it is only through the eyes of "sick souls" like Leonard Cohen, David Bowie, and Damien Hirst that one is able to encounter the true depths of reality. Their unique aesthetic sensibilities do in fact push the faithful and faithless alike toward a crisis of faith, but it's a crisis of a particular type that operates in a different register.

All told, then, Freud was right to critique the kind of religion that functions as little more than a form of pathological self-delusion. But Freud overstates his case, for just as the visual art of Damien Hirst; the pop music of Cohen, Bowie, and Cave; and even TV horror stories like *Stranger Things* have demonstrated, the problem of self-deception is not unique to religion. It's a fundamentally human problem. So to say that readers of this book might have a crisis of faith (or become "sick-souled") is neither to abandon religion as wholly delusion nor to advance a "healthy-minded" religion that eschews existential angst and glosses over the incongruities of life. Rather, it is to suggest that, whether religious or not, we all need to undergo a conversion of sorts—a transition that will involve not only the betrayal of our dogmatism and the loss of our certainties, but also a new kind of openness toward the world.

Toward a Faith of Crisis

It is better to go to a funeral than a feast.
For death is the destiny of every person,
and the living should take this to heart.
Sorrow is better than laughter, because sober reflection is good
for the heart.

The heart of the wise is in the house of mourning,
but the heart of fools is in the house of merrymaking....

So I recommend the enjoyment of life,
for there is nothing better on earth for a person to do except to
eat, drink, and enjoy life.
                                        —Eccl 7:2–4; 8:15 NET

It's one thing to acknowledge that life is complex. It's quite another to make existential angst in the face of death the central preoccupation of one's faith. But it is something else altogether to understand the experience of divine absence as the necessary condition for any faith at all. To put it in these terms is not simply to reverse the theism/atheism binary, but to upend it entirely. It is to suggest that what Christianity needs at this moment in time is not so much a crisis of faith, but a faith of crisis. And if this is indeed the case, then a number of promising avenues immediately open up within the contemporary cultural context for pursuing exactly this kind of faith.

First, a faith of crisis is one that always starts with the catastrophic—the traumatic real. And in fact, it never really moves beyond this original point of departure. In many important respects, contemporary life can best be understood as fundamentally post-traumatic. What this does not mean is that people have simply experienced in the now-distant past some traumatic event that continues to exert its influence on their lived experience today. Rather, it means that they are living in a constant state of retraumatization on both individual and societal levels. The catastrophic effects of the death of god surely ripple out into every domain of human life, but the existential angst caused by this state of godforsakenness is only compounded by repeated traumas that seem to constitute the contemporary situation: mass shootings, violent acts of terror, global financial meltdowns, sexual assaults, systemic racism enacted by the criminal-justice system. The list goes on and on.

A new set of coordinates is therefore needed, and the primary point of origin is the trauma that gave birth to the world of modernity—the severing of the sacred and the secular. Importantly, though, to locate a faith of crisis firmly within the catastrophic is not to give in to a despairing nihilism. It is not to signal the end of the world. Rather, it is to make way for its beginning.

Second, a faith of crisis acknowledges that some gods simply need to die. The reason the life and death of Jesus was, is, and continues to be so scandalous to so many different groups of people is not simply that Jesus (and his followers) claimed he was God. What is far more scandalous is that Jesus's death by crucifixion signals the death of all gods. It thus constitutes a crisis unlike any other, especially for those in positions of power. It's why the imperial hierarchy and the religious establishment both agreed that Jesus had to be executed, for whether religious or political, power traffics in absolutes and zero-sum games. By its very nature, power is in the business of making totalizing claims upon those who wield it and those who are oppressed by it. In doing so, power seeks deification. It wants nothing less, which is why a faith of crisis responds to power dynamics not by replacing one powerful god (e.g., religion) with another (e.g., science), but by taking up the posture of Jesus,

> who though he existed in the form of God
> did not regard equality with God
> as something to be grasped,
> but emptied himself
> by taking on the form of a slave,
> by looking like other men,
> and by sharing in human nature.
> He humbled himself, by becoming obedient to the point of death
> —even death on a cross! (Phil 2:6–7 NET)

This early Christian hymn is not merely describing the death of a man who claimed to be God. It is picturing the death of the death of god—the pouring out of divinity from God's very self. This divine emptiness has been woven into the fabric of the Christian faith from the very start. Christianity is a faith that is fundamentally a/theistic because it renounces any and every god that would regard divinity (and the power that comes with it) as something to be grasped.

Third, to embrace a faith of crisis is to recognize that religious faith in the modern West (especially Christian faith) is already in a crisis. The religious landscape of North America is markedly different from its European counterpart, but the numbers remain striking. It isn't simply that religious practice is in decline. It's that an increasing number of individuals no longer identify with any religious tradition whatsoever. Indeed, those who are entirely unaffiliated (i.e., describe themselves as "atheist, agnostic, or 'nothing in particular'"[8]) constitute an ever-expanding portion of the American population. These demographic shifts reveal a number of interesting trends regarding the modern crisis of faith in the West, but they are by no means cause for despair or resignation. Rather, they simply highlight the fact that, in an increasingly post-secular world, the only kind of faith that can be sustained is a faith of crisis. For only a faith animated by the aesthetic vision of a/theism will have the capacity to engage this massive cultural conversion in terms of the opportunities it presents, and to do so without descending into despair and despondency over the loss of faith that will likely become a defining feature of the contemporary cultural imagination.

Finally, a faith of crisis is one that has its feet planted firmly on the ground—in the muck and mire of a tragicomedy that none of us started and none of us will bring to a conclusion. Abstract philosophical speculation has its place but remains largely unhelpful and otherwise beside the point if it does not in some way speak directly to the concrete realities with which human beings grapple on a regular basis. Concrete artifacts in popular culture, whether music, visual art, or television, embody and express the basic desires that motivate contemporary persons to action and around which they orient their lives. In so doing, they give voice to the core trauma that continues to haunt us all, making its presence known even (and perhaps especially) through its absence. Which is why it seems only fitting to give the final word to a few a/theists who have articulated in aesthetic form that which exceeds the limits of the prosaic and the propositional:

Why has thou forsaken me?
    —Leonard Cohen, "The Guest"

Lord, my God, who am I that You should forsake me?
    —Mother Teresa of Calcutta, *Come Be My Light*[9]

My God, my God, why have you forsaken me?
    —Jesus, quoting Psalm 22

Notes

1. Mother Teresa, *Come Be My Light: The Private Writings of the Saint of Calcutta*, ed. Brian Kolodiejchuk (New York: Random House, 2009).

2. Sigmund Freud, *The Future of an Illusion* (New York: Norton, 1989).

3. Our discussion of Freud and James has been influenced by the work of Richard Beck, especially *The Authenticity of Faith: The Varieties and Illusions of Religious Experience* (Abilene, TX: Abilene Christian University Press, 2012).

4. "[Healthy-minded] religion directs [the believer] to settle his scores with the more evil aspects of the universe by systematically declining to lay them to heart or make much of them, by ignoring them in his reflective calculations, or even, on occasion, by denying outright that they exist." William James, *The Varieties of Religious Experience: A Study in Human Nature* (London: Longmans, Green & Company, 1906), 121. As Beck puts it, "healthy-minded religious experience is [according to James] ... a form of instinctive self-protection against emotional disturbance. This protection is accomplished through repression and denial. It is an intentional form of blindness in the face of life to produce positive affect and existential equanimity." Beck, *Authenticity of Faith*, 114.

5. Beck, *Authenticity of Faith*, 115.

6. James, *The Varieties of Religious Experience*, 140.

7. Beck, *Authenticity of Faith*, 116.

8. "To be sure, the United States remains home to more Christians than any other country in the world, and a large majority of

Americans—roughly seven-in-ten—continue to identify with some branch of the Christian faith. But the major new survey of more than 35,000 Americans by the Pew Research Center finds that the percentage of adults (ages 18 and older) who describe themselves as Christians has dropped by nearly eight percentage points in just seven years, from 78.4% in an equally massive Pew Research survey in 2007 to 70.6% in 2014. Over the same period, the percentage of Americans who are religiously unaffiliated—describing themselves as atheist, agnostic or "nothing in particular"—has jumped more than six points, from 16.1% to 22.8%." Pew Research Center, "America's Changing Religious Landscape," May 12, 2015, https://tinyurl.com/ybwocqcm.

9. Mother Teresa, *Come Be My Light*, 186.

Index